THE HEART AND SOUL
OF THE THERAPIST

---

*Rage, Fear, Desire, Loss, and Love
in the Psychotherapy Relationship*

Stephen Howard, MD

D1566437

University Press of America,® Inc.
Lanham · Boulder · New York · Toronto · Plymouth, UK

Copyright © 2008 by
University Press of America®, Inc.
4501 Forbes Boulevard
Suite 200
Lanham, Maryland 20706
UPA Acquisitions Department (301) 459-3366

Estover Road
Plymouth PL6 7PY
United Kingdom   '

Library of Congress Control Number: 2007943668
ISBN-13: 978-0-7618-4012-1 (paperback : alk. paper)
ISBN-10: 0-7618-4012-5 (paperback : alk. paper)

For my most beloved:
Arlene, Marisa, Isadora and Emmett

For all the colleagues and clients
who have taught me so much

And finally, for my friends and collaborators in the
American Academy of Psychotherapists

THE HEART AND SOUL OF THE THERAPIST
Rage, Fear, Desire, Loss and Love in the Psychotherapy Relationship

Contents

FOREWORD
By Larry Schor, PhD

To open a new book and begin reading is to enter a moment pregnant with possibility, and perhaps even risk. Will the work offer new understanding? Will I be challenged, entertained, enriched, engaged, or maybe even influenced by the words I am about to read? Who is this book written by, and for whom is it written? The answers to these questions as well as the questions Dr. Howard raises in this book are simultaneously simple and intricate; obvious and subtle. Therein lies the paradox of *The Heart and Soul of the Therapist*.

Stephen Howard is a psychiatrist and this book is presumably written for others of his creed. But wait; the less obvious and more telling description is that he is first and foremost a psychotherapist in an age in which psychiatrists are trained to avoid personal relationships with their patients and rely largely on psychotropic medication to alleviate symptoms of mental illness. His observations, insights, illustrations, and guidance are grounded in almost forty years of deep psychotherapy practice, preceded by a period as a general medical officer and a tour of duty in Vietnam with the Marine Corps. Dr. Howard is intimately familiar with the terrain of human suffering and healing; he has engaged personally the ethical struggles around living and dying.

This book, therefore, is written for anyone whose profession involves therapeutic work with human suffering. Whether one is a psychologist, social worker, counselor, marriage and family therapist, graduate student or seasoned professional, this work offers insights into the power of human connection as the essential agent of therapeutic growth. You will not find techniques or procedures "found to be efficacious through randomized clinical trials." The premise lies in understanding *being* rather than *doing*—how to be, and how to be with, our clients and patients rather than what we do for and to them. Our actions grow from our personal presence in the relationship.

Dr. Howard asserts that while psychology is a science, psychotherapy is an art informed by both science and intimate personal experience. In the consulting room we experiment with courage, honesty and presence, rather than with independent variables occurring in a sterile laboratory.

There are many ways to illustrate the difference between artist and technician. Countless weekend workshops are offered promising participants competence in this or that method of therapy. Likewise there are weekend workshops in guitar-making. By Sunday, you leave with your very own guitar. On a deeper level, the crafting of a fine musical instrument requires knowledge and understanding of physics, materials, acoustics, emotion, and even music itself. Here the therapist is the instrument and the therapy is the music. As Dr. Howard states so clearly, we often play our music for an audience of one and our work is the "specialized form of the art of relationship."

Thus the development of the therapist is a lifelong journey and Dr. Howard provides essential maps describing the territory. Peppered with explanatory and evocative vignettes, the student/apprentice will appreciate these clear examples while the experienced therapist will undoubtedly find thoughtful connections to his or her own experience.

This book happily raises more questions than it answers. Consequently, it will be subject to criticism for offering apparently cursory discussion of important themes like suicide, addiction, money, and ongoing training. Like any worthwhile endeavor, considerable investment is required of the reader to access the full depth of the work. For example, Dr. Howard endorses the fourfold dictum to, "show up, pay attention, tell the truth, and don't get attached to outcomes." These principles sound easy enough, but like any discipline, involve considerable examination and self-understanding. "Telling the truth," for one, implicates a range of self-disclosure from responding to personal questions to the possibility of saying to a client, "I can understand why no one likes you."

As someone involved in the training of psychotherapists, this is the book I have been waiting for, and wish had been a part of my own preparation. It invites the reader into the real world of therapy. It is already influencing my teaching and deepening my learning around the challenges embedded in therapeutic relationships. It will be equally rewarding for experienced psychotherapists seeking new vitality and freshness in their work.

Like psychotherapy itself, the reader will reap the greatest benefit by investing as fully as possible in the relationship with what is being read. Ultimately, the outcome will not depend exclusively on "how good the book was," but also on the depth with which the reader engages it.

Larry Schor, Ph.D.
Associate Professor and Coordinator of Therapeutic Services
Department of Psychology
University of West Georgia
Carrollton, Georgia
October 2007

PREFACE: A CONTEXTUAL NOTE

I am a psychiatrist, and the work has been a joy to me. But the designation "psychiatrist" now has a different meaning than it once had.

Today the majority of psychiatric training programs concentrate on biomedical issues, advancing little interest in psychotherapy. They offer a great deal of technical knowledge, but are too often devoid of wisdom about people or about life. Not long ago, by contrast, most psychiatrists considered psychotherapy to be the essence of the work. The attitude at Boston University, where I began training in the late 1960's, was essentially: "OK, Doc, while you're here learning to be a good psychotherapist, don't forget to pay attention to the medical aspects. They are also important, and someone has to do it."

The Psychiatry Department at Boston University was filled with very bright men and women who were highly skilled at psychodynamic (also called psychoanalytically oriented) psychotherapy. This background in analytic thinking provided a superb place to begin a career, and an excellent base to build on. Yet I had questions from the beginning. My personal experience and my undergraduate work in philosophy and religion had left me deeply impressed with man as a creature in relationship. This perspective infused everything I learned, and impelled me to re-think and reframe it step by step.

This conviction of the overriding importance of relationship has served me well, both as therapist and as teacher. Through the theoretical conflicts and the deluge of ideas about therapy, this vision has lighted my way.

It a source of sadness and grief to me that the vital work of psychotherapy is no longer seen as being in the psychiatrist's domain, and that the great majority practices as if psychiatry were a branch of internal medicine. There seems little room here for intuition, mystery, life experience, or the awe and power of meaningful relationship. Consequently I have identified myself increasingly as a psychotherapist rather than a psychiatrist.

In 1981 I was fortunate to be invited to join the Atlanta Psychiatric Clinic. This was a distinguished group with a long history, first as "outlaws" in academia, then as the spearhead of some original directions in therapy. It was this group in which Carl Whittaker began, and it included Thomas P. Malone, Richard E. Felder, and other people of fine mind and heart. I will always be grateful for their friendship and mentoring.

Their main thrust validated and refined the relational one that had been guiding me. Calling their approach "experiential," they had been practicing and teaching this way of thinking for years. I learned much from them, and remain deeply in their debt. The fifteen years I spent practicing with this group left me enriched beyond expression.

My other professional and personal windfall came in 1991, in the form of the American Academy of Psychotherapists. This interdisciplinary group of therapists maintains a steadfast focus on the person of the therapist, insisting that what we do professionally is a direct manifestation of who we are personally. This brave and creative band of people has been my community, my spiritual base, and an ongoing source of growth and stimulation. My gratitude to—and joy in—this organization knows no bounds.

Stephen Howard, MD
Atlanta, Georgia
September 2007

INTRODUCTION

We sit in small rooms day after day, immersed in other people's lives, sometimes lonely in the process. Unlike a singer or dramatist, we perform our art for an audience of one, or perhaps two, or a small handful. Even this audience has come not from interest in seeing us perform, but out of its own pain, need and hope. They scrutinize us intensely, sometimes seeing more of us than we might like, at other times not seeing us at all. We try to cultivate self-awareness, discipline, compassion and wisdom. But we are human, all too human, and we often fail. Usually they forgive us.

Such is the strange practice of psychotherapy. It presents us with irreducible ambiguities and mysteries, perennial conflicts and problems. When we think we are on top of things, we are usually about to be surprised. It is a profession of challenges and difficulties, endless variety, and frequent moments of delight.

The practice of this profession confronts us with recurrent questions, inherent enigmas that cannot be ignored. We must reflect on the nature of this unique relationship, the problems of working within our own limits and anxieties, our ability to tolerate love and hatred, and the continual striving for a vision that transcends our own personal perspective. We are obliged to make unceasing decisions about the use and abuse of theory, the conjunction of spiritual and psychological viewpoints, and the place of neuroscience in psychotherapy. It often feels like catching water in a sieve, over and over.

However, if one pays attention, one may learn a few things in thirty-eight years.

I have had the astounding good fortune, and the awesome responsibility, of spending a long career practicing psychiatry and psychotherapy. It has been endlessly fascinating and challenging, taking me to settings as diverse as hospitals, universities, a prison, a public health clinic, a drug rehab program, and a busy and rewarding office practice. I have also been privileged to teach and mentor. Ongoing education is crucial: psychotherapy is a boundless and complex art, intense and personal and intimate. It takes years to learn. No one ever masters it completely, and we are always practicing. The students and working therapists I teach have repeatedly urged me to put my experience in print.

My aim in writing is both broad and deep. Psychotherapy is a living process, a relationship in which two or more people engage for the purpose of fostering fundamental change. I hope to portray the depth of intimacy, of joy, and of personal risk that this entails, rarely depicted in the professional literature. The work you hold in your hand (or read on your screen) is a labor of love.

It is the fashion today to "proceedurize" psychotherapy, viewing it as a series of maneuvers or behaviors that one can memorize, categorize and apply. We are advised to make a medical-style diagnosis, and then consult the manual to see which remedies to apply. And quickly, please.

We are urged to work within the current political and economic climate of "managed care." The term itself is a shameless oxymoron. The people who come to us need to be honored and cherished, not managed. This profit-driven system fosters a corruption of the healing art, a surrender to market forces. Changes in culture, commerce and social structure are—and should be— reflected in what we do. But psychotherapy must investigate and illuminate these changes, not be ruled by them.

In these thirty-eight years, I have never had the same hour twice. Every client is special, every family is different, every therapist, situation and relationship is unique. When I supervise other therapists, I don't tell them what to do; I suggest ways to think, to relate, and to draw on their own resources. This book springs directly from those thousands of hours of clinical supervision, workshops and instruction.

I cannot tutor you "how to do" psychotherapy any more than the art teacher can inform you "how to create" a painting. The best learning and teaching of this art, like all others, occurs in a close mentoring relationship. One becomes a therapist by way of being an apprentice, and throughout our careers we return to that position as we consult our colleagues to solicit their advice, support and direction. Professors, journals and books can give us useful ideas and information; they cannot teach us what to think or how to relate.

At the opposite extreme, psychotherapy can be portrayed as a mysterious venture, an esoteric and purely intuitive territory that lies beyond description or rational understanding. This view also is misleading. The truth is that *psychotherapy is no more and no less than another human relationship, albeit a very special and remarkable one.* It is that unique and curious alliance that this book addresses.

I have tried to speak to some basic questions: What actually *happens* in psychotherapy? What do we do, and why? How do people change, and how do we influence those changes? What are the rewards and the dangers of practicing this curious art? And how do we take care of ourselves in the process?

You will find here little theory and even less technique; the emphasis is on the events and experiences of this singular relationship, and on the person of the therapist. It is not a compilation of research, but an attempt at psychotherapeutic wisdom. Consequently, I hope and expect that practitioners of diverse schools of thought may all find something here that is worthy of their reflection.

PART ONE

HEART AND SOUL

CHAPTER 1
PSYCHOTHERAPY AS RELATIONSHIP

Relationship and Experience

Jerry squirms a little in his chair, looking uncomfortable. I address his discomfort. "You made that remark casually, but I think this must be very frightening for you."

"Well... yeah... I guess so."

"Is it? Scary, I mean?"

"Um... well... actually, I do feel scared, now that you mention it."

As gently as I can, I ask him, "That was hard to say, wasn't it?"

"Uh-huh. I didn't even know I was scared until you asked me. How did you know?"

"As I was listening to you I felt a knot in the pit of my stomach and a lot of tension in my arms and shoulders... as if I expected to be hurt."

Tentatively, he asks me, "You're saying I'm expecting to be hurt?"

"That's my guess. I know I feel scared for you."

He looks puzzled, so I add, "I would be scared if I were in your place. An awful betrayal in your marriage, all these years of living a solitary life and not exposing yourself, and now you're opening yourself to a relationship again. Why wouldn't you be fearful? It's only natural."

"You'd be scared too?"

"You bet. You've protected yourself for a long time, and now you're dropping your guard. I get scared when I let myself be that vulnerable."

For the first time today, he smiles. "It's OK?"

"It's OK."

He looks relieved.

"Is that what you do?" I ask, changing the subject slightly. "You don't let yourself know what you're feeling?"

"I guess so. Is that a bad thing?"

"You miss a lot of information that way."

"Information?"

"Yes. When I pay attention to what I'm feeling, I get all sorts of clues about what's going on."

That leads us into a discussion of emotions. Jerry has not been accustomed to paying much attention to his feelings. He knows how to be angry or resolute, but the more vulnerable emotions are a bit of a mystery to him. It is only after this that we return to his fears about his new relationship. When we do, the discussion has a different tone, one that begins to take account of his inner state. It has also become a venue where he and I can share our experiences of longing, fear and change; we're in this together.

•

Darla has been talking about the abusive marriage she recently left. Her pain hangs in the air, palpable enough to tangle my fingers in. I tell her that.

"Can you really understand that?" she asks. "You're not a woman."

"Darla, you know I've been to war. I know what it is to be hurt and terrified, and to feel helpless and out of control. The situations are not the same, but I think the feelings must be very similar. But you're right; I can't completely know what it was like for you. Thanks for trusting me with it anyway."

•

These short dialogues present a vision of psychotherapy different from the one to which many people are accustomed. Here the therapist may speak of his own experience, both outside and within the therapy office. He reveals some of his own feelings about the client's experience and about the client (doing so thoughtfully, not indiscriminately). He mostly expresses himself in ordinary language, using little jargon and few technical terms. He imparts insights that he has struggled to learn, and he is free to express some of his own uncertainties. The interpretations he offers are in the form of questions, hunches and suppositions, to be tested against the client's experience. The separation between him and the client is one of learning, experience and responsibility, not one of higher authority. He makes no pretense of being fundamentally different from the people he is treating.

This is undeniably a relationship, if an unusual one. The two are not on equal footing; one is a professional therapist, the other a client. Yet there is a fundamental equivalence: that of two people in relationship, sharing the struggles, aches and joys of living. Other important relationships—of parent and child or of mentor and student—are also unequal; but they are mutually caring and reciprocal, and they involve the full presence of two authentic persons.

•

The phrase *psychotherapy as relationship* does not denote a theory of personality, a set of techniques, or a prescription for doing therapy. Relational psychotherapy is a way of thinking about the many deeply personal ways we influence clients and are influenced by them. It is a direction of thought useful to therapists of varying theoretical schools and clinical approaches.

That inclination has led me to a view of psychotherapy that is divergent from much current thinking. The writing and teaching of psychotherapy today is, on the whole, procedural, prescriptive and technique-oriented. It is rare that attention is given to the unique and intimate experience of the therapy relationship or to consideration of the therapist as a person with needs, motives and a life to live. The focus in this work will be on the nature of this relationship, the effects of this bond on the therapy, and the decisive presence of the therapist as a person. It is a personal and collaborative way of thinking about what we do.

The notion of personal experience is central to our considerations. Experience—the experience of both client and therapist—is the basic information from which we work. This data takes precedence over theory, technique, and even beliefs about how psychotherapy should be done. Sometimes our experience doesn't match our theories; when that happens, it is time to reexamine our theories.

Life is often difficult, and so many of our difficulties are forged in the experience of relationship. The events of relationship birth our traumas, our vulnerabilities and our strengths. In the most fundamental way, these experiences shape the persons we are, helping to create the *self*.

Experience involves the entire person, the whole *self*. The idea of *self* is holistic; it includes emotion, thought, sensation, spirit, intuition, wonder, action and relationship.

Some experience leaves us troubled, causes us pain, or prevents us from realizing the fullness that life might afford. Some experience gives rise to disconnection, obsession, dissociation, dread and all the other ills that bring people to our attention.

Notwithstanding our ideologies and explanations, we are left with one inescapable fact: *The only healing for experience is new experience.*

Here is one good way that we can define our work as psychotherapists: *It is our task to provide the opportunity for special kinds of encounters, so that new experiences may lead to the healing of old wounds.*

Radical Relatedness

This task of facilitating new and healing experiences can be realized only in the domain of relationship.

The philosopher Martin Buber spoke of a relational imperative in human life. He described two modes of existence: the first he called *I-it*, in which I see the other as an object or a function. I buy an item at the store counter; the clerk rings up my purchase and says thank you. Her mind is elsewhere. I smile in her direction and move on to my next errand. Neither the clerk nor I have seen each other as persons. She and I are *it* to each other.

The second mode he called *I-Thou*; I address the other as a *person*, encountering a *person* whom I honor. This *person* stands out for me against all the human and non-human background; this *person* is, in my eyes, unique, individual, irreplaceable and sacred. This *person* is not the means to some end, but an end in himself.

Buber goes on to say: "...the I in the basic word I-Thou is different from that in the basic word I-It." In more prosaic language, we are one kind of being in encounter with living *persons* and another when relating to objects.

This vision of our humanity suggests a view of the self that can be thought of as *radical relatedness*. It expresses a deep conviction that *any understanding of human existence must include relationship as an aspect of one's self and identity*. One's relationships are integral to selfhood in the same way as lungs, eyes, brain or a sense of wonder. My relationships are a facet of who I am as much as my height, smile or love of music. No account or description of a person, however detailed and extensive, can be complete without including the rich matrix of connections within which one's life is embedded.

I was working in the emergency room when a dying man was brought in by ambulance. He had suffered a heart attack and gone into cardiac arrest on the way to the hospital. We began the resuscitation, but after a while saw that we were not going to get him back. I pronounced the time of death, and a strange suspension of motion set in. Something was missing. A sense of anonymity and disconnection pervaded the room. It wasn't until his family arrived and reacted to the news that his death became wholly meaningful. Both his existence and his death were incomplete without the impact they had on the people who cared about him.

We miss much if we look only within the individual, without reference to his or her relational context. On the other hand an exclusive concentration on the externally observable, as sometimes seen in behaviorism and systems theory, will likewise be inadequate.

The notion of radical relatedness is simply this: *We are individual creatures whose singularity must be appreciated and cherished. At the same time, we are each the locus of a rich web of connections and relationships that equally define our identity.* These two statements are complimentary, not contradictory.

In quantum physics, scientists ask whether a photon (the subatomic unit of radiant energy) should be seen as a particle or a wave. One set of equations clearly describes it as a particle, while a second fits wave characteristics. Accounting for the photon's behavior requires both descriptions. So which is it? Is it a wave or a particle? The physicist would answer: Yes, both. Logic may seem to contradict that answer, but reality doesn't much care for our logic. If the facts don't fit our theories, we must rethink our theories.

The idea of radical relatedness requires us to employ *binocular vision*, the vision achieved when two eyes see together. Hold your hand a foot or so before your face. Now close your left eye and observe that hand only with the right. Without moving your hand, quickly switch eyes. Because perception depends on the position from which an object is observed, each eye yields a slightly different image. It is only with the simultaneous use of both eyes that we gain a vision in depth.

An integrated, binocular view of the human condition begins with our willingness to perceive with both eyes simultaneously, to apprehend a person as both a precious singularity and as part of a rich fabric of connections. Anything less and we are Cyclops, the creature with one eye, lacking depth perception and easily blinded.

The Relational Imperative

Life is often difficult, and too frequently painful. Some of its sorrows are an unavoidable part of living: loss, limitation, aging and death. Some are random misfortunes: disease, accidents and natural disasters. There are those afflictions imposed by others, from obnoxious neighbors to murder and genocide. And there are sufferings caused by distortions of our psyche. This latter group we think of as psychopathology.

I admit to some discomfort with the term "psychopathology." The relationship to physical illness is inexact; it smacks of a medical model that can be discordant with human experience. We could equally speak of emotional illness, difficulty, disorder, affliction, distress, disturbance, confusion and conflict. Perhaps we can come up with a better term; if you have an idea, let me know.

The idea of radical relatedness leads us to a conclusion about psychological distress: psychopathology does not occur only within the individual. It has its genesis concurrently in the relational sphere and in the intrapsychic one. To say that simply, *all psychopathology is forged in the crucible of our relationships.* In relationship we develop our strengths and our vulnerabilities, our anxieties, conflicts, inspirations and guilts, our hopes and fears, our most basic attitudes about our world and ourselves. In our relationships we become optimistic or pessimistic, gregarious or reticent, assertive or retiring, insecure or self-assured.

I do not mean to discount biology. Anyone who has spent time with newborn babies can tell you that we are endowed with different temperaments, capacities and inclinations. But these, like intelligence or height, are ranges of possibility, not fixed quantities. A child may be born with a tendency to be sensitive to the emotions of others; his relational experiences might incline him to be an actor, a diplomat or a psychotherapist; they could also render him a forlorn recluse or a pitiable appeaser of people.

Since all pathology is formed in relationship, then healing must occur in the same context. *The therapeutic relationship must be the healing container, the agent for change, the medium of personal repair and growth.* All the events of the therapeutic endeavor emerge in the relationship between client and therapist: symptoms, resistance, insight, distortions, conflict and collaboration, trust and suspicion.

It is not helpful, for example, to say, "The client is resistant." It is not that the client resists some arcane process, or even some insight. *She is resisting something about our project together.* Perhaps she is embarrassed, fearing I will shame her. Perhaps she feels I am being too bossy, pressuring her to do something she is not ready to do. Maybe she doesn't trust me. Or she could be experiencing divided allegiances: if she tells me what is on her mind, she will feel disloyal to her husband. I must honor the resistance as important and necessary. If I do, either the resistance will diminish or the discussion will lead us to areas even more fruitful than the original one. In either case we will be building trust and alliance.

Thus we arrive at a cardinal rule, one with only the rarest exceptions. *Whatever else is happening in the therapy, if something bears on the relationship, drop everything else and pay attention. Attend to the relationship first and always.* Unless the building is burning, nothing is more urgent. It is the relationship that is always immediate and present.

Jake is telling you about some difficulty with his manager at work. As he expresses his annoyance about an arbitrary rule, you realize that his words could also apply to the fact that you recently charged him for a missed appointment. If you pursue the overt content, sorting out his relationship with his boss, something present and immediate may be missed. Instead, you venture your hunch and ask him if there is anything to it. With some reticence he admits to having painful feelings about that incident; he knows it was fair for you to charge him for your time, yet he feels injured by it. Not only is this full of meaning in his relations with others; if you do not explore it with him it will sit between you, a silent saboteur in your path.

As soon as we sit down today, I am impressed with how appealing Sallie looks, her black curly hair falling to her shoulders and a flush to her skin. While I certainly have noticed how attractive she is (I'm not made of wood), it doesn't ordinarily claim my attention like this; today I find it distracting. A few minutes later she is telling me about the young psychologist she met at a party last Saturday. She found herself powerfully attracted, and has had several erotic fantasies about him. After listening respectfully, I wonder why she is going on about this right now. When she begins to reiterate her fantasy, I gently interrupt to comment that there seems to be a lot of sexual energy in the room today, and something about a psychologist. Sallie blushes, embarrassed and pretty, and we get down to her fear—and desire—that I may want to be sexual with her. I don't tell her about the rules; I simply tell her that if I did such a thing, I wouldn't be able to live with myself.

People enter our offices bearing their lives in their mouths, offering themselves in exquisitely tender and anxious ways. Frequently the most important themes come alive in their relationships with us, and they must trust us to be alert for such events. These are some of the most powerful and fruitful moments available to us, and we don't want to miss them. Once again: *First and always, attend to the relationship.*

The Person of the Therapist

The client has come to us because something in her life has become painful and disappointing, and she doesn't know what to do about it. She only knows that something must change. If she knew how to accomplish this herself, she wouldn't be here.

At this moment only one thing in her life is different: she has begun a relationship with a psychotherapist. *The therapist, and her alliance with the therapist, must be the agent of that change.* Nothing else is available.

As with all of us, certain patterns, cycles and interactions have become part of her life. She behaves in particular ways, expects and generally gets specific responses, and in turn replies in ways that are long established. The easiest thing for us to do is to enter into her accustomed style with her, participating in her established patterns.

Cindy conducts her life in ways that invite others to protect her like a child. She will do the same with me, and I may respond by trying to take care of her. I have made this mistake many times; I think most of us have. I may be acting from my own parental instincts, my desire to be kind, or my wish to be a hero.

When I allow this to happen, there will be no change. We merely repeat the stereotyped exchanges that are already making her unhappy. If I wish to be helpful to her I must stand outside her habitual arena, answering her invitation in a different way. I might simply decline to respond; I might ask her how others react to this behavior. I might tell her she is prompting my impulse to take care of her, but that I don't think it would be respectful of me to act on that invitation; I would be treating her as though she really were incompetent.

How would I know to do this? By experiencing my own desires and using them as information. By utilizing my experience and my supervision to help me see the relational context for these feelings of mine. But above all, *by being myself.* I have learned to behave in some different ways in my life, and I have experienced the dangers of falling into caretaking behavior.

We are now in a position to make our most extravagant claim of all. In a very real way, we can say that *therapy is about who we are when we are with our clients.*

By being ourselves, by utilizing the persons we have become and can become in our professional and personal lives, we present this sufferer with a new relational experience. Through this experience her habitual ways become conscious, opening the possibility for questioning, for realizing consequences, and for testing alternatives and seeing herself differently. Cindy may now begin to understand that her dependent behavior invites disrespect, renders her ineffectual and subservient, or unacceptably constricts her life. In the interaction with her therapist, she can begin to see and try out different ways of behaving and being.

The implications for us as therapists are similarly radical. It means that *our first and ongoing task involves our own growth and integrity as persons.* If we play a role or follow routinized and prescribed behaviors, if we respond to our clients with a lack of consciousness, if we give in to ego or greed, lust or competitiveness, we are certain to repeat some of her damaging experiences.

These statements open some very complex and interesting considerations, and we will devote the next chapter to them. Before we do, there is one more topic to take up. This one is intrapsychic—the other eye in our binocular vision.

The Unconscious

Sigmund Freud got some things wrong, but many things right. Today it is easy to discount him and some of his ideas; this is often done in disregard of the intellectual, social and historical context in which he worked. Yet his thinking represented a radical breakthrough in our understanding of ourselves, and the impact of his body of work must be ranked with those of Newton, Darwin, Marx and Einstein. Many of his concepts have become foundational for modern psychology and psychotherapy.

Perhaps the single most significant of his new hypotheses was that of the unconscious mind. He often wrote of "the Unconscious" as if it were a thing, like a pancreas or a gall bladder. Of course it is not a thing but a concept, perhaps a metaphor. A bit of cultural history may be helpful here.

European and American society in the nineteenth century remained dominated by the philosophy of the Enlightenment. This ideology saw humanity as fundamentally rational, and held that the advance of reason was leading to inevitable progress in an ordered universe. Countercurrents—such as romanticism—had arisen, but the predominant thinking remained rationalist. Science, particularly Newtonian physics, seemed to reinforce these ideas of progress and order.

By the early twentieth century the rationalist train was beginning to come off its rails. The notion of enlightened humanity had been boldly challenged in the philosophies of Nietzsche and Kierkegaard, and in literature by writers like Dostoyevsky, Conrad, Baudelaire and Rilke. In physics the works of Einstein and Heisenberg introduced relativity and indeterminacy into the science that had seemed to promise a predictable universe. The post-impressionists and cubists brought subjectivism and relativism into painting, while Durkheim and Weber explored the irrational elements in society. Perhaps the final blow came with the advent of the Great War of 1914-1918; the madness and carnage of that bonfire made it almost impossible to believe that humanity behaved reasonably or sanely.

In the midst of this commotion there appeared a Viennese neurologist with his studies of dreams and hysteria, demonstrating inescapably that human motivation is regularly dominated by forces that are not only outside of reason, but even outside of consciousness.

Today we take it for granted that much mental activity goes on below the level of conscious awareness, and that our lives and behavior are deeply influenced by this dynamic. Of course we can't perform a dissection and put our hands on "the unconscious," but it makes a most convenient way of thinking about all those unseen influences.

Freud viewed the unconscious as a seething cauldron of dangerous impulses and drives, the two primary forces having to do with sex and death (*eros* and *thanatos*). He believed that socialized living depended on the suppression or sublimation of these drives. Unfettered, they were menacing, nasty and destructive, and civilization itself would collapse in chaos should they be loosed in their raw form.

The horrors of the World War seemed to support this view. Although Freud had been writing and publishing his theories since the turn of the century, it was in the cultural despair that followed this war that they gained vast popularity. The unprecedented butchery and generally perceived meaninglessness of this catastrophe went a long way to shatter the earlier faith in progress, rationality and the essential goodness of humanity. Freud's gloomy pessimism fit the times perfectly.

Perhaps in reaction, Carl Jung saw the unconscious as a wellspring of generativity and healing. Jung had recovered from several years of his own psychosis, and had forged his experience into wisdom. His vision was further colored by his deep spiritual inclinations. He saw unconscious forces as full of potential for growth and creation, and he welcomed their liberation.

The tension between these two views has run through the world of psychology ever since. Which one you choose probably depends more than anything else on your own temperament. I suspect it's a projective test or a self-fulfilling prophecy—the unconscious becomes what we think it is. If we are willing to treat it as creative and healing, it is likely to be creative and healing.

For several reasons, attention to unconscious forces and motivations is vitally important to us as therapists.

First, any psychotherapy that ignores this dynamism will bring about, at best, external change. There are legitimate occasions for exhortation, behavioral conditioning and intellectual correction of "faulty premises" or "distorted thinking." All have their place, but the changes they produce rarely go very deep. If they did, we would simply advise people as to what is good for them and they would do it. The success of that approach is demonstrated by the fact that today no one smokes tobacco, uses dangerous drugs or has unsafe sex.

Secondly, one of the key processes in psychotherapy must continue to be the unveiling of unconscious material. As this material comes to consciousness, we can begin managing these inclinations and making deliberate decisions about them. This will be taken up in some detail in Chapter 3. For now, we simply observe that *we are helpless to do anything about matters of which we are unaware. Consciousness must be the first step in any intentional change.*

CHAPTER 2
THE HEART AND SOUL OF THE THERAPIST

"Our art demands the whole person!"
Carl G. Jung

The Therapist as Agent and Resource

When the client enters your office, he is longing for change. Baffled and inarticulate about what this change could be, two things in his life offer hope at this moment. The first is consciousness of pain; he is experiencing some sort of loneliness or heartache. The second is that he is here, in your office. He is making a connection that he hopes will provide the relief that he can't find elsewhere else in his life.

This relationship is not only the setting but also the agent of change. If something new is to happen, it will begin in this alliance. That's all we have to work with. This seems so obvious that we must wonder how it gets overlooked.

The individual we designate as "client" brings to the relationship all that he can bring. If the endeavor is to lead to anything new, it will depend on the difference that we introduce. That cannot be simply a matter of technique. While our knowledge and technical skills are important, the fundamental difference depends on what we bring as persons. It is in this sense that the therapy is about who we are when we are with our clients. *It is the appropriate use of the therapist's self that provides the lever for change.*

The "use of the therapist's self" means that we make available to the process everything about who we are. We enlist it all: not only intellectual knowledge, but also feeling, intuition, experience, personal history, caring, insight and empathy. This is fundamental to doing psychotherapy in a relational manner.

Appropriate attention to our own being implies issues of integrity, relational responsibility, personal congruence and knowledge. Let me elaborate.

The word *integrity* derives from *integer*, meaning unitary, single or whole. When we approach our clients with integrity, we bring our entire selves, our strengths, uncertainties, resources, vulnerabilities and mortal follies. This does *not* mean that we reveal everything; that would do violence to ourselves and to the client. It does mean that we are fully present, willing to encounter this person as one genuine human being to another.

Entering such a relationship entails responsibilities: we are responsible for our compassion, honesty, self-awareness, energy and benevolence. There will be times when we are not able to meet these responsibilities; we must own that limitation also.

Carl, a very capable pastoral counselor, left City Hall and arrived at my office for the weekly meeting of his supervision group. His marriage of four years had just been dissolved in court. He felt certain that divorce was the right thing to do; nevertheless, it was an agonizing experience. In the course of venting to the group, he mentioned the clients he had scheduled for the afternoon. Someone asked him whether he was in any shape to see clients. He replied that they were on the schedule and it was too late to do anything about it. We insisted that not only *could* he do something about it, but he *must*. It would have been irresponsible to those people, as well as to himself, to see them when his own resources were so depleted.

The importance of the therapist's integrity implies the need for *congruence*. By this I mean that I will do my best therapy when I work in ways that are compatible with my own character and inclinations. If I tend to be orderly and organized, it makes sense for me to do orderly and organized therapy. If I go about things in an untidy but intuitive way, that is how I will work best with my clients. If a particular approach is in conflict with my disposition or my values, that is an approach I'd do best not to take.

You will not do therapy quite like anyone else, because you are not anyone else. Students and therapists will often try on a style or technique that they observe. They may be modeling a teacher, a mentor, or someone they see at a conference. This is a natural learning process; you may need to try on many coats in order to find a few that fit. But keep in mind that there is no "right" size or cut of coat, only the ones that suit your own frame. The therapy that you do must be congruent with your character, values, personal style, strengths and weaknesses, ease and inhibitions, and intellectual and emotional capacities. It is crucial to honor our different levels of comfort regarding—among other issues—formality, self-disclosure, displays of emotion, touch, or discussions about religious matters.

The use of self provides a wellspring of knowledge. We all have our stories, and our own lives become resources. We bear our wounds and the adventures of learning to deal with those wounds. We know about struggle and triumph, pain and doubt, loss, friendship, longing, love and loneliness. We can carry these things into the therapy we do, enriching our empathy and learning, strengthening the bond of common humanity between our clients and us.

Giving free reign to our associations, fantasies and intuitions will supply us with a wealth of information. Carl Whittaker used to tell of falling asleep during a session. He would have a dream, then wake up and relate it to the client. This apparently worked for Carl, but I don't recommend it. I wouldn't have the nerve. Still, waking images can work in exactly the same way.

Sitting with clients, I frequently have visual images that are rich in meaning, and I often share them. I might say to someone, "Listening to you tell this, I have a picture of you in a small boat. You're rowing away like mad, but the shore doesn't get any closer. You look weary." This conveys to her in a graphic way something about my perception of her situation. It may lead her to understand how tired she is, or to see that she is trying to do something she can't do, or to reevaluate where she wants to go.

There are countless things going on at any given moment in a session. It would be impossible to attend to them all, and many are unconscious. We cannot always know what we are communicating through body language and other non-verbal means, nor can we read all the messages being sent our way. We cannot know just what the client is taking in, and an event to which we attribute little importance may be momentous to him. Our own mental connections may be obscure to us. We have flashes of insight and intuition, often coming inexplicably from the recesses of our own hearts.

It is not possible to apprehend all this. It is not possible even to know all of what we ourselves are doing. We can only be who we are. We have no choice but to trust the wealth of material arising from the unconscious. We cannot afford to miss it; like radar, it spots obstacles and provides guidance.

When I speak of bringing one's whole self to the therapy, I don't mean to suggest indiscriminate chatter, nor do I wish to violate the therapist's life and privacy. Bringing one's entire self concerns the therapist's awareness, wholeness and attendance, and not necessarily his behavior. It means a willingness to be fully connected and to care. It means that the therapist allows everything about himself to enter into the relationship, overtly or not.

How much to share with the client is a very individual question. I am at ease revealing a great deal, but that may not be right for you. I suggest that you reveal as much as you can be comfortable with, *as long as the material seems likely to serve the client's needs*. It may be useful to him to hear how you felt or behaved in a relevant situation, or how you are experiencing him; it will not be helpful to hear about your financial worries, your jogging program or the difficulty you are having with your partner in the office. Nor is it always wise to speak everything you are thinking about the client; you may be wrong, or he may not be ready to hear it, or the context may be misleading. Honesty does not entail total transparency, nor does it excuse a lack of judgment and critical thinking.

There are some fundamental attitudes on the part of the therapist that will serve both parties well. These include caring, acceptance, a degree of humility, and intellectual and personal curiosity.

There must also be the willingness for self-discipline and thoughtfulness. Over the years, many forms of pseudo-therapy have been offered to us. These include ill-conceived and poorly run encounter groups, undertrained "counselors" espousing an ideology (religious, social, or political), and coerced short-term therapy (even some graduate schools have come to bow to the monetary interests of the health insurance industry, teaching methodologies based on market economics rather than repair and healing). The common element in these "therapies" is a set of unproven and superficial premises about human psychology, combined with a lack of emotional and intellectual discipline. It invites impulsive and even thoughtless behavior on the part of the therapist, especially when events take him outside his areas of competence, or when his own needs become involved. There is an unspoken pretense that mere goodwill and a few manipulative tricks can promote recovery and well being. The truth is that quality psychotherapy requires as much personal and intellectual discipline as the practice of internal medicine or architecture. We must understand human nature and utilize our training and experience to provide a healing environment based on the client's needs.

It is also important that the therapist enjoy his work and his clients. If there are more than brief periods when this is not the case, one should search carefully for the reasons. The remedy may be as complex as changing the work environment, or as simple as needing a vacation. It may be that the therapist needs to learn better self-care (see below). This work is intense and oftentimes difficult, and if we are not deriving pleasure from it, both we and the work will suffer.

There are many things that can make this work fun. There is endless variety; no two clients, or even two sessions, are the same. There is continuous intellectual and personal challenge. We learn about people and their lives, the world's most fascinating subject. We get to have intimate relationships with a lot of interesting folks. And it allows us to make a living in a way that is satisfying and meaningful.

Finally we must consider countertransference. This is a complex issue that deserves its own section.

Transference, Countertransference, and Experience

Our experience teaches us what the world is like. If we have been treated kindly and have had our needs met, we will see the world as a friendly place, worthy of optimism. Experiences of frustration and deprivation lead us to expect frustration and deprivation.

This is equally true of our relationships. We expect to be treated as we have been treated in the past. Chaotic or unpredictable kinships teach us not to trust or depend on others, even while aching to do just that. Kindness and reliability prepare us to expect the best of others.

On one level, transference is that simple: *we expect, consciously or unconsciously, to be treated as we have been treated.*

Carlos's father was harsh, demanding and challenging with him. Nothing Carlos did was ever adequate or acceptable, and the boy endured constant virulent criticism. At the beginning of our relationship he would pause repeatedly to explain and defend himself. When I told him I didn't need him to do that, he was bewildered and mistrustful. It was difficult to believe that he did not have to justify himself to me, that I was glad to accept him as he was. A large part of our therapy has consisted of testing this assertion, revealing himself slowly and vigilantly observing my responses. As he becomes convinced of my acceptance, he is learning that he is acceptable and worth caring about.

In psychoanalytic terms, Carlos and I have addressed the transference distortions. In the language of experience, we have had a long period when he grappled with a kind of "double vision", seeing me in the mold of his father and simultaneously seeing the person that I am with him; the person he expects and the person he is experiencing. I have not behaved as he anticipated, and this has been a revolutionary experience for him.

Transference feelings and perceptions are extremely powerful, having their genesis in formative relationships. Their appearance invests the therapist with a potent relational force; in Carlos's mind I have all the authority that his father once had. The therapist must treat this authority as a trust. It can be powerfully healing; abused, it is terrifying and destructive.

The original relationship, when it reappears in the transference, is most often that with a parent, though other important people show up. The relationship may not be with a specific person, but with a group or institution that teaches the child about the nature of things, or about right and wrong. It might be a school, church or ethnic community, or social expectations in general. If my religious upbringing, my family, or my community has informed me that sex is degrading, I will carry this into my life and my therapy. The therapist's differing view may be my first opportunity to see things otherwise.

The power of the transference enables some basic things that we do in therapy. One of these is modeling. I address a surly teenager with non-punitive clarity, demonstrating for his parents a different approach. With another client I mention the mid-day break I take, using the time for lunch, catch-up, and relaxation; this is valuable to him, for he is just beginning to learn that he is a person aside from work.

Another use of this transference authority lies in the messages we deliver. Some common examples:

"Your emotions are important."

"You are allowed to say no."

"You are worth caring about."

"Your feelings here are only natural."

These are the sorts of declarations we hopefully deliver to our children as they grow. We are saying similar things to our client because he has not heard them enough from *his* parents; the transference allows us to repair that deficiency.

Equally as important is the occurrence of our own responses. In the course of the relationship the therapist experiences a broad range of emotions, thoughts and impulses. He may feel kind, generous and loving, and at other times find himself angry, envious or impatient. Some people are difficult to care about. Some are provocative. All are complex, and our responses may be complicated.

These feelings arise within us based on the actuality of the current relationship. They occur in the present situation, and we can usefully refer to them as *counterexperience*. In addition, we will have our own countertransference feelings and distortions. Like everyone else, we carry some of our expectations and attitudes from other relationships into this one. I may find in this person echoes of a parent, sibling, lover, or other figure in my life. The client may be an object of my projection: I see in him some quality of my own that makes me uneasy; he tells lies, and I used to do that. Or my own needs and vulnerabilities lead me to act out a role that the client unconsciously assigns to me.

If we are to avoid reacting blindly, these effects must be acknowledged. *When I find myself having difficulty with someone's therapy, it is most often because I have not come to terms with my own attitudes and reactions.* The opportunity to recognize and manage our own responses is the single most valuable part of consultation and supervision.

I had been working with Ursula and Mack for a year. Their inability to have children had been a highly emotional issue for both of them. Our therapy had gone well at first, but lately we seemed bogged down. Every idea, every suggestion or insight, somehow failed to bear fruit; the womb was barren. They were still blaming each other and fighting ferociously. I felt baffled and frustrated, and had to bridle my impulse to blame them in turn.

They accepted my suggestion that we invite a consultant to join us. I chose Doug, one of my practice partners, because his style was so different from mine. For several sessions he listened to the three of us talk about their life and our therapy, and made comments as things occurred to him. I don't think anything he said made much impression on the couple, but it prompted me to see some things about my place in the puzzle.

By our next meeting, I had done a lot of thinking. I said to them, "Doug helped me understand what has been happening here. Ursula, in your dependent behavior you have been taking the role of the child you never got to have. Mack, I think you've been playing the part of the daddy you never got to be. And I've let myself become the adopted child who's been brought in to save the marriage. My taking on that job hasn't been helpful to the two of you, so I want to tell you that I'm resigning as of now. From here on I intend just to be your therapist."

I don't know how much they understood, but that wasn't the important part. My behavior changed. I was no longer caught in the same static repetition, and they were invited to try something new. The work began moving again. The problem had not been with them, but with me. The obstacle had been my own countertransference, carried over from a childhood role that I'd thought I must assume.

In much of the psychoanalytic literature, countertransference has been viewed as something undesirable, a land mine to be avoided. When it does occur, analysis of the therapist is required in order to "resolve" it, that is, to make it go away. But countertransference does not just "go away." *Countertransference is the projection onto the client of our expectations, based on our own earlier history.* It is as inevitable as weather, and it need not be destructive. If I have grown up taking care of those around me, I can expect caretaking to be a recurring impulse. I may act on this inclination, throwing my projections across their paths like stones. Or I can attend to my impulses as important information, a compass that helps me find my way.

Countertransference will occur, and the important question is whether we identify and manage it creatively and in the service of the therapy.

Attending to our reactions to the client, both countertransference and counterexperience, gives us valuable insight. I had been seeing Brenda every other week for three years, and we were wrapping up. Today would be our next-to-last session.

Our adventure together had been quite successful. She had ended a chronically unhappy marriage, accomplishing this in a loving and respectful fashion. Now she was leaving town to begin graduate studies at seminary. In setting out to become a minister, Brenda was fulfilling a desire she had held from her youth but put aside when she married.

At some point in the conversation I noticed—for the first time—that she had lovely legs. Huh? I hadn't taken notice of her legs in three years, so why now? I quickly took my mental pulse, and didn't think it was my own erotic distraction. Then I understood. For a long time I had seen Brenda as a girl, just as she had seen herself. My notice of her sexuality was a tribute to the womanhood that had blossomed in her. She was delighted when I shared this insight with her.

All sorts of feelings may inform us. I rarely find myself bored in therapy; when I do, I can be pretty sure it's because nothing is happening. I might venture, "You know, I'm usually intent on what you're saying. But today I find my attention wandering. I wonder if what you're talking about is really what's important to you right now?" This question usually results in an immediate, if slightly embarrassed, change to a subject that is anything but boring.

If I am feeling impatient, it may be that she is encountering some unrecognized obstacle, perhaps something she is hesitant to talk about. If I feel irritated, there is a good chance I am being provoked. These feelings furnish valuable signals about what is going on in the relationship. Since our emotions are so much quicker than our thoughts, these clues may come long before we could think things through. Our hearts are typically much smarter than our brains.

The fruitful management of countertransference and counterexperience depends on our willingness to be conscious about our motives, intentions and behavior. That consciousness may not be important in flying an airplane, selling hardware or taking out a gall bladder, but it is essential in psychotherapy. It could not be otherwise, since the therapy takes place in an intimate relationship in which people profoundly influence each other.

Ethical issues arising in therapy are deeply influenced by the therapist's vulnerabilities and temptations; not the least of these take place in the countertransference. *Most of our ethical lapses and misjudgments stem not from a lack of knowing what to do, but from the temptation to do something else.* If we are not mindful of these temptations, we are likely to act on them. There will be major blunders, including transgressions motivated by greed, by sexual desire, and by our longings for power, adulation or affection. At the least, we will render the therapy ineffectual, since some of the client's adversities will play into our own blind spots.

The management of temptation, including countertransference challenges, depends on self-awareness. This is not always easy. Hopefully, time and experience increase our consciousness of ourselves and others; but this will happen only if we are willing to be reflective and unsparingly honest with ourselves.

Whatever heightens awareness of our own feelings and motivations is likely to make us better therapists. This includes all sorts of reflection and meditation, and there is no substitute for quality consultation and supervision. As we develop our ability to be with our clients and simultaneously monitor ourselves, we bring the art of psychotherapy to its highest state.

And once again, there is the therapist's own psychotherapy. The need for that should be obvious at this point, and I will not belabor it. Let me simply say that I have concerns for any therapist who has not engaged in fairly extensive psychotherapy of his or her own.

The Care of the Therapist

I have a favorite metaphor: I envision a bucket of water. We may dip from the bucket and pour water for someone who thirsts. This is a gift, freely given.

On the other hand, if we continually dip from the pail while doing nothing to refill it, it runs dry. After that, anything more is offered from an empty container.

There are two ways to prevent the bucket running dry. We may refill it, and we may slow the speed at which we empty it. If we are to remain caring people, we must do both.

We refill the bucket when we nurture ourselves or allow others to nurture us, and when we attend to the needs of body, mind and spirit. We refill it when we take time for our own lives, when we engage in playfulness and humor with our clients, and when we make sure we are paid adequately. These things may be difficult for us, for we tend to be a sacrificial bunch.

Even if we refill it, the vessel will run dry if emptied too quickly. We are up against the problem of limitation. However caring and generous we might wish to be, we will have shortcomings. We cannot give without end. If we don't recognize those limits and draw boundaries to protect them, we will soon be of little use to ourselves or to anyone else.

We can respect our limits and preserve our integrity only if we learn when to say *no*. Only by apportioning what we give can we maintain the inner resources to be kind, thoughtful and caring. We cannot work unlimited hours, cannot be there for anyone who thinks they need us, cannot be of help to everyone in distress. We cannot always say yes. If I am able to say no, then when I say yes I can say it fully and freely, from the heart. Then I can be generous and loving about it. If I only say yes, never no, I am being sacrificial. My yes becomes self-destructive.

We must see to ourselves; on an airplane, parents are advised to secure their own oxygen masks before tending to their children. To have concern for ourselves is to preserve our capacity to care. The impoverished self can love only poorly; love flows best from the nurtured self. When I am not being sacrificial, I can *choose* to give. My giving is an act of generosity, springing from a full heart.

Sacrifice may begin as an act of love; a parent forgoes a meal in order that his children may eat. But when we live in an *ongoing* sacrificial way, the self becomes depleted. Then sacrifice arises only from obligation; the self is mal-nourished. The term "selfless sacrifice" is an accurate expression of this starva-tion. He who goes on sacrificing is pouring water from an empty cup; what comes out is emptiness cloaked as caring. Sooner or later we become exhausted and resentful.

An offering is a gift. We may offer assistance, advice or prayers. To offer is to *present*, related to the noun *present*, that is, a gift; or to the adjective *present*, to be here. Springing from the intact and nourished self, this gift or present may be creative, bountiful and tender.

An offering recognizes one's limits, and is not destructive of self. When limits are not acknowledged, the giving becomes sacrifice. This living surrender is self-destructive. It breeds resentment, and it finally becomes unloving.

Let us look at the words we are using. *Sacrifice* stems from the same root word as *sacrament* and *sacred*. Its religious origins are clear. In the ritual sacri-fices of ancient societies, the sacrificial animal was slaughtered on the altar be-fore the people and God, and then burnt. That which is sacrificed ceases to exist. It is destroyed and consumed. If we speak of self-sacrifice, then it is the *self*, or something about the self, that ceases to exist. At the least, it is an alienation of one's own nature.

The word *selfish* means self-absorbed, narcissistic, satisfying one's own de-sires to the disregard of others. Unfortunately, the term is often misused to in-clude behavior more accurately described as *self-caring*. Self-caring is very dif-ferent from selfishness. *Caring for oneself and for one's own needs, loving oneself, does not require a disregard for others, only an equal regard for one-self.*

Someone will ask: Isn't self-love another name for narcissism? Well, no, not really. In the mythical story of Narcissus, this beautiful young man was ut-terly self-absorbed. He scorned the love of others, including the devoted Echo. Finally he fell passionately in love with his own image in a pond, and sat pining for it until he died. We can only hope that he will be happy together.

Note that Narcissus was not yearning for a person. He was yearning for an *image*. He was too much in his own thrall to *love*; instead he was *in love with* this image. When we are *in love*, we are absorbed in the object of our infatua-tion. Narcissus was absorbed with his own image and only his own image; love of others (or even self) was unknown to him. Narcissistic self-absorption is en-tirely different from tending to our needs as whole persons, which include lov-ing and being loved. Self-caring means simply that I too am a person, that my needs are also important, that my integrity and wholeness should not be sacri-ficed.

We are enjoined to "love thy neighbor as thyself." Not *more than*, but *as* thyself. As we love ourselves we become more capable of loving behavior to-ward others. Loving others is an act of the full person, of the intact self.

Today I felt overwhelmed by my practice. It has been extraordinarily busy, and the telephone calls have been constant. It seems that everyone suddenly needs something. "My son is home from college and I'm worried about how he's behaving." "Jack and I have been fighting for three days. We need to get in to see you right away." "I was doing fine but today I had another anxiety attack; please call me right away." "My medication isn't working right!" "My cancer doctor upset me today and I need to talk to you."

I've been resolutely sticking to my scheduled appointment times, refusing to book extra hours or give up my lunch break. As usual, folks somehow get through until I can attend to them. But this morning I found myself irritated over something I would normally laugh off; it was clearly time for some self-care. Taking advantage of a cancellation, I blocked out an hour to return calls when nothing else would compete for my attention. I told my secretary not to book any new clients for at least a few weeks—longer if it remains this busy. And I made sure to leave on time to go to the gym.

Just pushing on while ignoring my limits would be disrespectful to my clients and to myself. The quality of the work would deteriorate and everything would suffer, including my personal and home life. It isn't selfish to know when you've reached your limit. *Taking care of yourself is good therapy for your clients.*

Supervision

No amount of learning and contemplation will give us perspective in every situation. We will always be subject to our own distortions, temptations, fatigue, ignorance and fallibility.

I may not see the client's issue because it is too close to home. Gina is trying to tell her husband that certain behavior of his feels disrespectful to her. I don't get what she is telling him because of the similarity of my behavior. Certainly I never behave disrespectfully.

We find ourselves in areas where we are blind. We require someone else to look in, to provide vision and perspective. At this point in my career I am usually the teacher or the supervisor. Yet I meet regularly with senior colleagues for invaluable peer support and supervision. Without it, my work and my clients would suffer.

Supervision—whether individual or group—provides a place where the therapist can let down her hair, be vulnerable and even ignorant, and receive sustenance and support. She can expect collegial support, ideas, ongoing education, and help with issues theoretical and practical.

This requires trust. In supervision as in therapy, the best work will occur only when it is safe to expose oneself. We need the qualities in our supervisors that our clients seek in us. The attributes of the best supervisors include compassion, tact, patience, honesty, self-awareness, knowledge and experience, and the desire to teach and to challenge. To this I would add, as with the good therapist, a sincere interest in the welfare of the other person.

Supervision should provide an occasion for the therapist to expand his vision, effectiveness and enjoyment of the work. In keeping with our relational focus, the purpose of supervision beyond the student level is not to "teach one to do therapy." The intent is to provide a relational experience that promotes growth as a therapist and as a person. It is an exciting opportunity to learn together. The content and process of each supervision will be unique, varying to meet the character, experiences and needs of each therapist and group of therapists. The relationship between supervisor and supervisee is best described as mentoring —a combination of coach, tutor, friend, guide and, yes, therapist.

I am aware that my use of the word *therapist* invites disagreement. There are those who insist upon a sharp delineation between supervision and therapy. For the most part, I agree. When the therapist is ready or needful of psychotherapy, this should be undertaken separately.

Nevertheless, supervision must in some respects be therapeutic. The therapist wishes to expand his ability to relate well and to be himself while in relationship with clients and families, and this sometimes requires dealing respectfully with relevant personal issues. The intent of therapy is increased richness and quality of life, while the aim of supervision is increased richness and quality of therapy.

This touches, again, on the issue of self-care. As a group, we psychotherapists tend to be caretakers, people who assume excessive responsibility for the well being of others. These habits have been adaptive in our original families, and hopefully we come to terms with them in our own therapy. I like to say that I began my career as a family therapist at the tender age of three. It didn't work out then, and I'm still trying to make up for it.

Family of origin influences, as well as self-care issues, arise constantly in our work, and therefore must be a significant theme in supervision. The therapist will sometimes resist the supervisor's confrontation of these problems, for they have very personal roots. The supervisor must approach the subject with persistence, respect and tenderness, modeling self-care for those he hopes to guide.

CHAPTER 3
HOW PSYCHOTHERAPY HEALS

In the original Greek, *psychotherapy* meant "healing of the soul." If we are serious about what we do, psychotherapy is still the practice of that healing. To *heal* is to make *whole*—and also to make *holy*, for all three of these conjuring words come to us from the same root. We work in the tradition of priests, shamans, medicine men and physicians. We join an ancient and holy calling, one that engages us in a sacred endeavor, requiring us to approach our clients with reverence.

As we set out to *heal*, we must think about something called *health*. It is not easy to say what we mean by that. The analogy to physical health is inexact.

Listening to therapists speak, some of the things we seem to include in the notion of health are self-acceptance, competence, the ability to form satisfying relationships, the living of a life that balances love, work and play, a degree of freedom from inner conflict, and perhaps something called "self-actualization."

This list is hardly exhaustive. Healing implies injury, and we hope to bring about some sort of repair, some sort of change for the better. The word *wholeness* seems to suggest our intent.

As our clients progress in their work, they re-create their lives. They begin responding to events in different ways, doing things they haven't previously done, and managing situations with new responses. They report freshness in their relationships, an increase in satisfaction, and a more coherent sense of self.

We see them exhibiting more vitality, speaking with increased assurance. They express pleasure with the changes. They say mysterious things such as, "Now I feel like the person I was meant to be."

Some of that change is not measurable. It does not show up on objective scales. Qualities of creativity, openness, generosity, personal contentment or the ability to love do not appear on behavioral charts. Nor does the experience of healing. Outcome studies are important, but there is much of life's meaning that they do not reflect. That which is not measurable may be profoundly real.

Counseling and Psychotherapy

The words *counseling* and *psychotherapy* are often used interchangeably. I suggest it would be useful to see them as different ways of bringing about change. The characteristics of the changes would be different.

In distinguishing between the two, please understand that I am not trying to match these words with anyone's formal discipline or with the nomenclature of licensing boards. Many people formally designated as Pastoral Counselors or Licensed Professional Counselors are—in the process discussed below—truly psychotherapists. I am talking about the processes, about what we may be doing at any given moment.

The process I am calling counseling is also referred to as psychoeducation. Synonyms for the word *counsel* include *advise, teach* and *direct*. Ralph has been having a difficult time with his new boss, a middle-level manager in a state agency. This is not a transference problem; it has nothing to do with other relationships in his life. He is simply new to bureaucracy and doesn't yet grasp the unspoken rules. Having operated in a similar environment myself, I think I see the problem and also some ways to cope with it. We spend the rest of today's session educating Ralph about how to work the system. This is counseling.

Counseling can be seen as a content-focused educative process, often directive. Ralph acquires knowledge and perhaps some new skills. Psychotherapy, on the other hand, is more about subjective experience; it is process-oriented and exploratory. Marc, also in conflict with his boss, has been struggling with authority problems arising from his unsuccessful attempts to satisfy his exceedingly demanding mother. This emerges in his relationship with me as well as with his boss, and we are engaged in the therapeutic endeavor of sorting out the transference.

I do not intend this distinction between counseling and psychotherapy to be taken as hierarchical; I am not saying that one is "better" than the other. I am saying that psychoeducation and psychotherapy are different processes that serve different purposes. In the course of a single session we are likely to find ourselves alternately doing one and then the other. Counseling mostly engages cognitive learning, while psychotherapy involves the entire person of both client and therapist. For the sake of clarity and brevity, let me put this in list form:

Counseling	Psychotherapy
left brain (cognitive)	whole brain (cognitive, emotional, intuitive, spiritual)
content is primary	process is primary
educative (teaching)	learning through relational experience
oriented toward behavior	oriented toward subjectivity
focus on external circumstances	focus on inner experience
directive	exploratory
linear	organic

solving problems	personal process
reduce anxiety	tolerate and learn from anxiety
emphasis on productivity	emphasis on quality
hierarchical	egalitarian
counselor as instructor	therapist as participant
new skills	new sense of self

Because of these differences, it is true that therapy is more complex, more difficult to learn, and requires more experience to do well.

The new learning that results from counseling is one important agent of change. For the rest of this chapter and the next, we will focus on some healing processes that are specific to psychotherapy. First, a few matters that tempt us away from the psychotherapeutic endeavor.

What Doesn't Work

Tyrone and I are in our fourth session. He tells me about a decision he has to make and I offer an observation about what it might mean to him. He looks at me keenly and says, "You're not going to give me any advice about this, are you?"

I smile and shake my head.

"I pay you all this money, and you don't give me any advice."

"Tyrone," I respond, thinking quickly, "Go out on the street and stop the first ten people you see. Tell them your story. Every one of them will give you advice. You pay me to do better than that."

He gets it. "So you don't think you can tell me how to live my life?"

"Nope," I say, "I'm not that smart."

Everyone will tell you what to do. Every citizen is an expert psychologist, philosopher, physician and baseball manager. If you don't believe it, take up the challenge I proposed to Tyrone. I promise, you will get more advice than you can tote in a pick-up truck.

I can't tell you what to do because I am not you. I can tell you what I might do in similar circumstances, but that may not be right for you. I don't have to live with the results, so my advice is cheap.

People know just how cheap advice can be. That's one reason we rarely take it. In fact, people will do almost anything to assert their autonomy. Hands on hips, the little kid in us says defiantly, "You're not the boss of me!"

We may even turn down things that we truly want if acquiring them means surrendering our pride or our autonomy. In political revolutions, people even risk death rather than allow someone else to rule them.

Telling someone what he or she should do is not therapy. In fact, it is anti-therapeutic.

Telling someone *how* to do something he *wants* to do is teaching and counseling. If I tell you *what* to do, you are liable to defy me. Or you may capitulate and secretly resent it, blaming me for any unfortunate outcome. Nothing wrong with you—that's just what we humans do. In either case I am making it difficult for you to work out what is truly best for you.

One popular school of thought advocates that we do "problem solving" or "solution-focused" therapy. Solving problems is a legitimate and helpful form of counseling; we teach a student a strategy for dealing with educational requirements, or we make suggestions as to how this woman can cope with her intrusive mother-in-law. But not everything fits the mold of "problems that have solutions." The fact that you own a hammer does not mean that every difficulty is a nail.

A problem-solving approach sometimes can be an unfortunate substitute for the hard work of understanding a deeper and more complex reality. In "problem solving" therapy, we are instructed to take the client's situation and work it into a cognitively definable problem, then direct the person in solving that problem. I suggest that you think about a quandary in your own life: a romantic relationship, a difficult decision or a family conflict. Now reduce it to an intellectually definable problem and then try to act on the logical (or the paradoxical) solution to that problem. Can you live with that? Neither can our clients. The very idea of "solution-focused" therapy carries its own contradiction: *good therapy is focused on clients, not on "solutions".*

In too much "solution-focused therapy", the determining operational question is this: How can I get my client to do what is expected of him so that he will produce the measurable result that his employer or insurance company requires? The highest values here are shrewdness and the perception—however ill-defined or unsupported (and whatever the cost) of quick results. Many difficulties in life defy our attempts to make them into solution-focused problems. It is disrespectful to imagine that we can simplify a person or a life in this way, discounting all the complexity and richness.

This contrived methodology is characteristic of the truncated and superficial "therapy" currently promoted by the health insurance industry. We are told to advise, direct and manage the people who come to us for help, setting goals for their therapy and doing whatever it takes to achieve those ends. In this artless, profit-oriented system, we are to engage in orchestration based on craftiness rather than on connection, caring and understanding. No opportunity is offered for relationship, wisdom, empathy, kindness, and the delightful ambiguity and abundance of meaning that makes life so interesting. Equally alarming, it precludes love, mystery and the sacred.

In the profession of psychotherapy, as in medicine or public service, we have accepted a sacred trust. Fulfilling this trust requires of us compassion, respect, thoughtfulness, and the openhearted wish for the good of the other person. Human beings don't need to be managed. Human beings need to be respected and loved, cherished and healed. It is often the lack of these qualities in our lives that brings us to therapy.

OK, I'll stop that now. Back to the vocation of healing.

●

There are many ways of thinking about what we do in psychotherapy. These include the psychoanalytic, psychodynamic, cognitive-behavioral, systemic, strategic, and numerous others. Each of them can be useful at different times, under different circumstances, and for different clients and therapists. No approach embodies "the truth."

Rather than dispute theory, I will try to describe some of the tangible healing elements that are present as we do therapy. These are much the same regardless of our beliefs, procedures or explanations. People will respond to kindness, caring, empathic insight or gentle humor with absolute disregard of whether we call their therapy cognitive-behavioral, systemic or psychodynamic. If they feel that we offer them respect, understanding and compassion, they couldn't be less concerned about our theories of personality, family structure, or therapeutic process.

I am not discounting technique, and will have more to say about that. I am saying that *all effective technique, in fact all effective healing, takes place in its relational context.*

The passing phenomenon of "Internet therapy" provides a good illustration of the shadow side of this position. Ill-advised attempts were made to provide what was essentially chat-room "therapy" to people who had no way of knowing better. This was—predictably—a dismal failure, enjoying a brief burst of semi-popularity and then disappearing like snow in May. No one was fooled for long. (This may change with the use of avatars and the projection of consciousness that this implies; that remains to be seen.)

Self-help books walk a middle ground. There are responsible ones that are useful, for example, in letting people know that they are not alone in their difficulties, or in giving folks some ways of thinking about their situations. The less responsible publications either mislead people with their generalizations and their counterfeit diagnoses, or offer exercises and prescriptions that are minimally useful outside of a relational context.

We will take a look at some of the healing events that actually occur in therapy sessions. These may be explicit or implicit, conscious or subliminal. The therapist's conception of the endeavor will influence the frequency and power with which these things occur. But even more so will they be influenced by the therapist's character and willingness to be in relationship.

Past Tense

If a man dwells on the past, he robs the present. But if a man ignores the past he may rob the future. The seeds of our destiny are nourished by the experiences of the past.

—Lao Tsu

The analyst sits behind the couch, stroking his beard and silently listening to his client. Finally he speaks, probably with an Austrian accent. He offers some abstruse interpretation based on the client's childhood traumas and his resulting complexes. The client leaps off the couch with a joyful exclamation, cured of whatever it was that ailed him after only twenty years of treatment.

This is an entertaining satire, and Woody Allen has made movies about it. But it isn't what most of us do. We've come a long way since the early days.

The opposite theoretical extreme is found in the work of some existentialist psychotherapists. Following the philosophy of Jean-Paul Sartre and others, they expound a radical freedom of choice. In that view we are always capable of totally autonomous decision. We decide at every moment who and what we are, and this makes us radically responsible for ourselves. The past doesn't matter. There are no excuses.

On one hand, this is refreshing. Too many justifications and defenses have been offered for bad decisions and bad behavior. We grow sick of the mentality that is always prepared to say "It's not my fault, and I'm entering rehab."

On the other hand, let's get real. Decision and responsibility are crucial elements of change, and we will have a good deal to say about them. But Wordsworth instructs us that "the child is father to the man," and he is surely right. The events and the milieu of one's early years have a great deal to do with how we perceive our world and ourselves, our possibilities and our limitations. My past experience tells me what to expect of life, what people are like, the nature of relationships, the range of available possibilities, and who and what I am. One part of therapy consists of becoming conscious of these perceptions and seeing that I do have choices. Until I am cognizant of what I am doing and of what alternatives I have, the idea of deliberate change is a chimera. What I don't know about cannot be a genuine choice. If I know of only one exit from this room, the other door is not a possibility. If I have been told all my life that I am stupid, it will require a new set of experiences before I can trust my own judgment. If I have never experienced benevolence, I may not recognize the possibility of choosing to be generous.

William Faulkner wrote, "The past isn't dead. It isn't even past." The past can never be simply irrelevant.

Marc (same hapless guy as above) views his work supervisor with great apprehension, fearing some awful punishment or humiliation if he doesn't please her. You point out to him that that's how his mother treated him, so it makes sense that he anticipates similar behavior from anyone else in authority. You wonder if he is expecting the same treatment from you, and he admits being fearful of that. At first this is just an interesting, if emotion-laden, insight. It is not change, only the first step in that direction.

He tests you in overt and subtle ways and finds you consistent; you don't reject him or punish him. He begins to believe in his relationship with you; over time this has a profound effect. It begins to alter his perception of himself. *No one ever believes that he is acceptable until he has had the experience of being accepted.* Marc at last begins to see himself as lovable. You have let him know that he is worth caring about in the only way that is meaningful: by caring about him.

Marc learned in his earlier experience that he was not worth loving for himself; it had to be earned. The only cure for experience is new experience, and in this current relationship new experience is occurring. By bringing the past alive in the present encounter, past and present can be held side-by-side, constructing a new vision. Marc's conception of himself is transformed, and this will have a profound effect on his life and his relationships.

Sometimes it's as simple as gaining a fresh perspective. "Your parents let you know that you were a lot of trouble," says the therapist. "How else would you think about yourself? You were just a kid. When we're kids, we think that the things our parents tell us about ourselves must be true." Taking this in over time, he can begin to say, "I thought that's who I was, but it's not about me. It's something I was taught. I see now that it was about their limitations, not my defects." He learns that the people who taught him were not infallible, and that the image of himself that they created is not one he must continue to live with. He begins to treat himself with greater respect.

At other times, reviewing the past has the simple purpose of making sense of one's story. Monica gets extremely anxious whenever Jack has to travel on business. She has alarming fantasies in which he never comes back. She keeps herself carefully in control, not wanting to make it his problem. She can deal with the anxiety, but it leaves her feeling that there is something very wrong with her, and it exhausts her.

The explanation offered her is straightforward. "No wonder you get anxious. Think about it. Your mother went on a short trip when you were six, and was killed in an auto accident. A few years later you learned to love your stepmother, and she died and left you. Of course you fear being left by the person you love the most. Nothing strange about that." This simple normalization of her distress gives her great relief. She still has her anxieties, but not because there is something defective about her. They are life's natural fears, and she is all right.

We may have the opportunity to overcome old fears. Janis has been unable to remain in a relationship with a man for long, however much she cares for him. As soon as things progress and he starts to speak of her as a part of his life, she becomes too anxious to continue.

The only child of a severely alcoholic mother, Janis became the companion for her weak and dependent father. He leaned on her heavily, not only to cook and keep house for him, but also for emotional support and personal validation. At the time it seemed that was just the way things had to be. It now becomes clear that she was overwhelmed by the responsibility, missing much of her childhood. Unconsciously she has expected to be similarly overwhelmed in any relationship today.

Not surprisingly, she begins to do little things to take care of me, her older male therapist. She is overly solicitous of my welfare, cautious not to upset me, and apologizes if she runs a few minutes over her time. I point this out and invite her in various ways to engage with me as one competent adult to another. Janis gradually comes to know that today she is not the child she was with her father. She can relate to a mature man who won't be dependent on her. She has resources today that her child-self never could have imagined. She can say no to expectations that she give more than is good for her. And she can get about her own life even if she is sharing part of it with someone else.

Examining the past can allow us to see context. Ella comes to our session today looking agitated. With great difficulty and apprehension, she tells me that she left here last week feeling angry with me about something I said. I listen to her and then agree that my remark sounded insensitive. I can certainly understand why it upset her, and I apologize for that.

Then Ella softens her words, backtracking, trying to undo what she has done. I reassure her that her anger did not harm me or frighten me, and she was entitled to my apology. I am all right and she need not take care of me, nor do I wish to retaliate. She finally gets it. "Oh," she exclaims, "you're really not like my mother, are you?" She can see that her placating and self-effacing behavior made sense in dealing with her capricious and unforgiving mother, but this is a different situation and it is no longer necessary.

In each of these accounts, the client gains a fresh sense of her own identity through her relationship with the therapist. She finds out that she can be different from what she has known. This is new learning, but a very different sort of learning than that which occurs in counseling. *This learning is not about skills, but about a new awareness of herself in the world.* When we understand that we are acceptable and lovable, we no longer need to shield ourselves in the old ways. We come to view ourselves differently, and previously unimagined possibilities arise.

Classical theory talks about resolving conflicts. But we don't "resolve" experience. Our experience is always with us. New relational experiences allow us to gain acceptance and understanding of the old ones, and thus to lessen their impact. While still part of us, these past experiences become more peripheral to who we are today. I often think that we are all crazy, and that sanity simply means learning about your own craziness and then making it work for you.

Present Tense

The psychoanalysts arguably have made the single biggest contribution to our thinking about psychology and psychotherapy. While it is easy to discount some of their original theories—penis envy and hysteria come to mind—other notions are foundational. If they had given us only the recognition of unconscious motivation, the importance of childhood in character formation, and the concept of transference, they would still be world-shaking thinkers. We take some of their notions so much for granted that we forget how radical they were in their time.

Nevertheless, if the existentialists have a legitimate charge against the psychoanalysts, it lies in the latter's extreme focus on the dynamics of the early years. The analysts have never been able to satisfactorily discuss change, freedom or self-determination. *Making the move from past to future involves development of personal resources, amplification of consciousness, and decision and self-creation.*

To begin with, there is the resource of intuition. A private detective once told me that a large part of his work consisted of women hiring him to find out if their husbands were cheating on them. Once they told him what they wanted, he said, the mystery was over: by the time they came to him they already knew the answer. But they had been taught not to trust what they knew, and thought they needed external proof.

Society teaches us the importance of "being reasonable" and "being nice." This can foster an unwarranted mistrust of intuition. While our intuitions are not infallible, they should always be explored. Giving ear to them makes available an important resource.

Vanessa has been separated from her husband for several months, and is in the process of filing for divorce. "I keep thinking," she tells me, "maybe I should give him another chance."

I must show my surprise, for she looks at me and says, "Not such a good idea, huh?"

I ask her what her gut feeling is telling her about that. She responds that she must have "given him another chance" twenty different times, and he has always disappointed and betrayed her. She still has a difficult time trusting what she plainly knows. But "another chance" would be the "nice" thing to do, and she was raised to be nice, that is, to ignore unpleasant truths and "be reasonable".

Our emotions, too, can be a resource. But they can also be a hindrance; we can spend prodigious amounts of energy avoiding our feelings, despite the fact that even unpleasant emotions do us no harm. The damage is created by the numerous things we do to avoid experiencing those feelings—everything from alcohol abuse to obsession, from dissociation to plain old numbing.

We think there is something wrong when we suffer pain, fear or sadness. But these perturbations are unavoidable elements of life. As we learn to endure them rather than fruitlessly trying to make them disappear, we can learn what they have to teach us.

One of the key emotions that we try to avoid is fear. Yet fear in itself cannot harm us, and the avoidance of fear can block our way. The truth is that you can do almost anything if you're willing to be scared while you do it.

The avoidance of anger can also be a detriment. Rosa has been afraid of her anger, and no wonder: in the large family where she grew up, two messages were heard repeatedly: that only bad people get angry, and that anger is very destructive. This devastating picture was painted with statements like, "How could you do this to me?" and "Your father will have a stroke when he hears this." A turning point in her therapy occurred one day when she was able to admit that she was upset with me. Speaking this aloud led to the discovery that I would not be destroyed by it, nor would I think badly of her. We could simply work out a disagreement.

Weeks later, having tested this proposition several more times, Rosa happily brought in a story. She had been at a business meeting to negotiate her agency's sharing resources with another agency. In the middle of the meeting she found herself growing angry without knowing why. Customarily she would suppress such a reaction; this time she called a break and went off to think. She realized that the other representative had proposed an arrangement that would put her at a considerable disadvantage. She hadn't been able to think it through that quickly, but her irate feelings had served as a warning system. Her anger also gave her courage to do something she previously would not have done: she returned to the meeting and told this man that his proposal was unacceptable and they needed to negotiate something more equitable.

In the therapeutic dialogue, we seek to amplify consciousness about ourselves and our lives. There is a (no doubt apocryphal) story about Sigmund Freud. A friend confronted him: "You psychoanalyzed such-and-such, and he's still an unpleasant son of a bitch." The good doctor allegedly responded, "Yes, but now he knows why he's such an unpleasant son of a bitch."

Insight is not healing in itself, but it is a step in that direction. Without mindfulness of our feelings, thoughts and motives, we are like a train on a single track; there are no alternatives to consider. I may not be aware that my behavior toward someone is edged with harshness. It becomes clear to me as I see my lack of kindness in my relationship with my therapist. Perhaps I realize that my hard feelings derive from another situation where they are more fitting. Becoming conscious of this perspective, I may wish to change my behavior. *Awareness is a resource that opens possibilities. One way we can think about therapy: it is the multiplying of possibilities and choices.*

Our new-sprung consciousness may concern the way we treat ourselves. Referring to her indifferent housekeeping, Elizabeth wonders what's wrong with her and why she is so lazy. She regularly tells me about herself in grimly judgmental terms like *lazy*, and I wonder whose voice we hear when she does that. Not surprisingly, this is her mother's valuation of her, currently reinforced by her husband. I offer to point out the instances in our conversation when she treats herself so harshly. When I do that, I suggest alternate explanations: it's understandable that she avoids housekeeping since she and her husband both work, he has resisted sharing the domestic load, and who likes housework anyway? She becomes increasingly conscious of her pattern of disparaging herself, and begins to look for more positive appraisals. She begins to hear my voice rather than her mother's, and to make it her own.

Future Tense: Decision/Creation

Therapy provides an opportunity to become conscious about our histories, and the effects of those events on our current lives. When we explore a transference relationship, we get to experience past and present simultaneously. We see that we need not be victims of past experience. We can make new decisions. We have alternatives to our behavior and even to our ways of thinking.

To be conscious is to expand imagination and generate options. We gain more choices about the persons we will be. On this point I agree wholeheartedly with the existentialists: we must account for freedom, decision, commitment and creation. Through the relational process, we have expanded our freedom. That freedom invites us to participate in creation, to affect our personal transformation. This moment of free decision is central in making change and moving toward the future.

Creation is available to all of us; it is not the exclusive province of gods and artists. The products of creation may include a child, a redeeming act, a poem, a kind word at the right time and a spouse well loved.

The products of creation may also include our selves. Years ago I read a passage in the Talmudic literature. The rabbis were discussing how one can become a better person. They examined aspects of will, grace, law, temptation and human nature. After the prolonged and exacting debates one finds in this source (rabbis just love to argue) they came to a deceptively simple conclusion: If you want to change something about yourself, behave as if the change has already occurred.

If I want to become more courageous, the rabbis advise me to act as if I were already brave. If I delay action while waiting for courage, I will be doing nothing but delaying action. Instead, acting in the face of my fear will engender courage.

If I wish to be kinder or more peaceful, I must work at it. Neither generosity nor equanimity will spontaneously appear within me. I must make a decision to do the generous or the peaceful thing. Once I act, the feelings will follow.

If you would like to be more loving, don't wait for loving feelings to occur. Look for the loving response in each circumstance. You become a more loving person each time you extend yourself, on every occasion when you reach beyond your own perspective to see the other's, and in any instance in which you choose the caring act rather than the reflexive one. When you do these things, you nurture love. When you have done this for a while you will find loving feelings blossoming within you. The emotions follow the choices and the behaviors. Grace awaits our decisions and our acts.

We like to speak of discovering ourselves, but that is only half of our story. We also create ourselves. Our customary behaviors express who we are; but *when we act from conscious decision rather than habit and custom, those decisions create the people we become.* To decide is to create. Shaping our own lives requires both self-discovery and self-creation.

Creation and discovery are interlocking processes. Following change, whether evolutionary or crisis-produced, I discover who I am. That is, I discover who I have become through the combination of my character, my history and my decisions. I discover the person I am today as I recognize new (or newly seen) behaviors, moods, and ways of thinking and perceiving. Creation becomes discovery and discovery again becomes creation.

Creativity is sometimes defined as the ability to see things in new ways. This, again, is true, but it is only half the truth. *Creation is also a process of finding new ways to become the people we wish to be.*

•

There is one more element of therapeutic healing that we must consider. It is arguably the most pervasive and important one of all: the experience of loving and being loved. We will take that up in the next chapter.

CHAPTER 4
PSYCHOTHERAPY AS AN ACT OF LOVE

Let's begin this discussion with a radical assertion: Love is humanity's single most powerful force for healing.

I am not being merely rhetorical. Along with our needs for food, shelter and rest, the need to love and be loved is basic to our being. Infants deprived of love often sicken and die; those that survive are likely to be permanently damaged. There is good evidence that the damage is neurological, that it becomes incorporated in the structure of the brain.

Love is no less decisive through the rest of our lives. There are few places where one has the opportunity to love and be loved in a safe and sustaining refuge. At its best, family is one of these. At its best, psychotherapy is another.

Acts of Loving

Philosophers and poets through the ages have tried to define love. No one has succeeded, for the good reason that love is not definable. Like God or childbirth, love is a sacred mystery.

We can, however, describe the characteristics of loving behaviors, and then see how they apply to our purposes as psychotherapists.

Loving acts have a number of attributes. These include connection, presence, acceptance, decision, wholeness, responsibility and generosity. The individual who acts from these attributes is creating love and bringing it to those he touches. Let's consider them one by one.

There can be no loving without *connection*. That is the first condition. But connection is neither easy nor safe. Connection implies caring, and caring makes us vulnerable. When we connect with someone, we place ourselves in danger of loss, injury, disappointment and pain. We make ourselves hostage to fate, accident and the will of others. Caring means that life will wound us. It is no wonder that we are often reluctant to love and to relate. It can be hazardous, and sooner or later it will hurt.

Yet there is no healing until we join with the other. In psychotherapy, this connection is the ground on which we stand, the fulcrum from which the lever of our personhood can cause someone's world to move. This cannot happen unless the therapist is willing to be vulnerable. *The client can benefit from the therapy only by being fully available to it. And the client can be fully available only if the therapist is present for his pain and his fear. In doing therapy, we are limited by what we are willing to endure.*

A second attribute of love is *presence*. In psychotherapy, both client and therapist must be as fully present as possible. The therapist must be conscious in the process, willing to risk, to be challenged, to be shaken from his convictions by the client's truth. This can be frightening; it does not permit us to become complacent or stagnant. It does not permit us easy answers, and it keeps us open to unbidden insights and to change.

A client stops at the end of a thought and says, "It's so good just to talk about this!" He is not simply letting off steam. He is speaking about not being alone, about having someone bear witness to his experience, and about having it affirmed in the eyes of another person. It's about seeing and being seen. It's about presence.

The quality of personal presence is so crucial that we will take it up at length in Chapter Seven.

Acceptance signifies the willingness to withhold judgment. This is the heart of all loving action. Not judging means that we embrace the enormous complexity, contradiction and imperfection of the other person. We welcome this person for who he is, putting no conditions or reservations on our acceptance. We make the assumption that being loved is his birthright.

When we do not accept and respect this complexity, when we do not receive the other in the intricacy of his personality and circumstances, when we insist on evaluating him by our own standards, then we cannot love him.

The acceptance that embodies love must be unconditional. "Unconditional" does not mean that any behavior is acceptable, or that you may abuse me. It means that my love need not be earned, that it is freely given. Perhaps the loveliest expression of this unconditionality that I've ever heard was spoken by my wife Arlene to our daughter as the latter was preparing to go off to college. "Marisa," she said, "Nothing you could ever do could make me stop loving you."

We commonly think of love as an emotion, a psychic event that springs forth spontaneously. In truth, love is not an emotion, nor is it something that happens to us. *Love is a decision, an act of will.* It is an active verb; we decide to love.

Love does not come about in a single decision, done once and for all. It requires an ongoing series of decisions. The other person does something that inconveniences me, or hurts my feelings, or angers or disappoints me. Each time I must make a choice: will I cast myself in the role of victim, or will I respond in a caring way? To love is to make the decision to act lovingly.

Because love is my decision, it may not be earned. It is my gift; I must give it freely, without condition or reservation, or it is something other than love.

Scripture commands us to love one another. There is nothing sentimental or romantic in this injunction, and nothing is said about how we feel. The entire Judeo-Christian ethic makes sense only if love is an act of volition.

Love is personal. We do not love objects, abstractions or things. People may be treated as any of these. We go through our day seeing most people as functions rather than persons. I step to the counter and make a purchase. The saleswoman hands me my change, smiles and says thank you. I move on. She has not seen me as a person, nor I her. We have dealt with each other as functions.

When I want to speak of love in its concrete, daily fullness, it must be *personal.* It must be about a *person* whom I honor. A *person* stands out against all the human and non-human background, unique, individual and irreplaceable. A *person* is not the means to an end, but the end itself, to be revered and prized for her very existence.

To love is to be responsible. The highest form of this is responsibility for oneself. We must be answerable for our own lives rather than blaming things, circumstances and other people. We must own our mistakes and lapses, and wonder what our part may be in any problem. It is not loving to hide behind authority or events. When confession and apology are indicated, we must do so in a straightforward way.

And finally, *love is generous.* When we love, we are willing to give. We place high value on the welfare of the other. To say this a little differently, we strive to overcome our narcissism, to transcend our natural self-absorption. Love multiplies itself; it is usually met in turn with love, for others and for oneself. Generosity interrupts cycles of self-protection, creating instead a mentality of abundance.

Love in Psychotherapy

The idea that the work we do is "value-free" makes little sense. Psychotherapy is not a disinterested investigation; it is a branch of the art of healing. We conduct ourselves very much within a frame of values; any other approach would be offensive. The attributes of loving behavior that we have described correspond with basic therapeutic values that we enthusiastically advocate.

The client should rightfully expect to feel the presence of the therapist, to identify the awareness, the close response, and the sense of being heard. In the midst of fears and discoveries, she should experience this guide walking closely by her side, sharing, empathizing and caring.

The therapist practices acceptance. He neither judges nor blames, and encourages the client similarly to refrain from judging and blaming. Hopefully the client feels accepted and embraced in her wholeness, including those elements that she thinks to be her weaknesses and sins. The therapist may question some of her behavior (so does she), but she can expect to feel accepted for who she is.

The therapist brings to the relationship his whole self, personal and intimate. And he remains responsible for his part of the relationship.

Generosity is integral to the therapeutic endeavor. The therapist values the welfare of his client. There are certain satisfactions we may legitimately expect from our practice, but the client's well being is paramount. It is the culmination of this generosity to allow her to leave us when ready, even though we take pleasure in her company and might prefer it to continue.

All healing occurs in the crucible of loving relationships, and psychotherapy is a loving relationship designed especially to facilitate that healing. Regardless of the theories and techniques employed, or the particular processes of any given moment, *the healing always occurs in the relationship*. That is why so many different personalities and approaches are likely to succeed: the healing power of the alliance may flow in many different channels.

Psychotherapy, properly conducted, is an art framed by these acts of loving. The loving bond works as a force for healing the psychic wounds that we all bear.

We all bear wounds because no one has had a perfect family life or an idyllic childhood; because the world wears at us, confronting us with disappointment, injury and frustration; because we never have all our needs met; and because even the good life includes struggles and losses.

Psychotherapy must be grounded in acts of loving because love is the only healing response we have in the face of injury, want, disappointment and strife. Because this is so, psychotherapy is a sacred venture and even a spiritual quest. This should not surprise us, for the original healers were priests, shamans and sorcerers.

The Practice of Loving

It's interesting to listen to good therapists of differing theoretical orientations. They describe the things they do in different ways, and their explanations are even more diverse. But when we watch them work, there are striking commonalties. The best therapists all act with respect, compassion, acceptance and presence. Regardless of their theories, these qualities stand out. When they do not, there is little healing.

One popular teacher of strategic therapy writes of his craft in ways that sound distant and manipulative, and he justifies this in his ideology. But I have seen him work. Although it is never mentioned in his descriptions, he brings tremendous warmth and empathy into the session. You can see people respond to this very personal energy. His prescribed methodology, in the hands of someone lacking these qualities, can create resistance or even frighten people away.

In psychotherapy we hope to teach people to love themselves better. *Only through the experience of being loved do we learn that we are lovable.* We can help people discover their worthiness only through our willingness to value their worth.

Loving people is not easy. It entails openness to our own changes, and also to risk, disappointment and loss. The therapist will sometimes have love returned but, like a good parent, may not depend on it or be motivated by hope of it. The therapist's satisfaction must lie primarily in the *acts* of loving.

As I hope I've made clear, loving is by no means all there is to psychotherapy. There is counseling, teaching, technique, use of the transference, opening of new resources, and all the rest. Yet my thesis remains: *loving acceptance is the necessary core of all healing.* Everything else makes up the suture that stops the bleeding and closes the wound. Only the experience of loving and being loved provides the vital force that actually heals.

There have always been therapists who have known this. Yet we have been reluctant to say so, perhaps because we are afraid of being seen as too soft and fuzzy. Traditionally our field wants to be considered rigorous and scientific. This has led to the use of terms such as "unconditional positive regard," as if that provided more clarity or more meaning than saying "love." Like most euphemisms, this expression is a pale shadow of reality. True healing takes place in the medium of a tender and loving relationship.

Psychotherapy as Parental Love

The act of loving occurs in many contexts and takes many forms. The love I bear for my mother will be quite different from the love for my dog or my best friend.

The love we bring to the therapeutic relationship will not look like romantic, sexual or conjugal love, or like my love of country. In truth, it will in most ways be analogous to the love of good parents for their children. For healthy growth, a child needs a mixture of nurture on one hand and discipline, guidance and supervision on the other. The balance varies with the circumstances and the child's needs and personality.

This is equally true for our clients. When we work with someone whose life and behavior is out of control—an addict, for example, or a troubled and rebellious adolescent—a hefty dose of confrontation (speaking the unpleasant truths) is in order, while we also attempt to teach him the power he can gain through self-control. Conversely, when the client is trapped in rigidity and repression, then nurturing, acceptance and "permission" to be himself are essential. Of course these are artificial separations. Good parental—and good therapeutic—care is always a mixture of teaching, limit setting, nurturing and acceptance.

The nature of the limit setting is important. Our task is to provide safe boundaries and structure within which the individual can explore and experiment. Neither the client nor the child needs us to engage in a power struggle with him.

Secondly, we hope—like good parents—to tend to the unique capacities, interests and needs of each person, the directions required by that individual's particular nature. This sort of nurturing signals a regard for the client's uniqueness that leads to the healing experience of feeling cherished and valued. When we offer this respect, we let the client know that we consider his aspirations and his life to be more important than having him take care of our needs. That may be a very different message from the one he received in his family.

Respect and love deeply affect our picture of ourselves. When we are children we see our parents as omnipotent and omniscient. The way they treat us is surely the way we deserve to be treated. Who they tell us we are is who we are, and this power is re-enacted in the transference. When parents treat us with respect and love, we learn that we are deserving and lovable. Many people have not had that experience; if they are to heal, they must encounter it with us.

And finally therapy, like parenting, is an endlessly repeating process of letting go, of allowing the child or the client to grow beyond her need for us. We begin to let go as we allow her to make her own mistakes and learn at her own pace. We let go when we accept that our notions of this person's welfare will sometimes be unsuited to her, and when we cease trying to rescue her, and whenever we assume that she is a capable human being. We let go when we are willing to acknowledge the world's capriciousness, to share with her the mystery, difficulty, joy and suffering that no therapy will ever eliminate from life. And we let go again at the end of therapy, when we accept the fact that she has grown and will be leaving us. As with child rearing, the course of psychotherapy is permeated with decisions about letting go and allowing her to be responsible for her own life.

The qualities of connection, acceptance, wholeness, creation and intimacy are essential to the fully lived life. They are equally essential to the fully healing psychotherapy.

CHAPTER 5
ON THE JOURNEY

Continuing our fundamental theme: The psychotherapy relationship provides healing experiences for the psychological wounds that life inflicts on us. All the events of therapy—insight, transference and countertransference, exploration of past and present, alliance and resistance and the rest—occur in the context of that relationship and are deeply colored by it.

The wounds have taken place in the past, but healing occurs in the present. The immediate experience, the one that is occurring here and at this moment, must always claim our primary attention. Whatever else is going on, it can wait while the relationship is served.

That remains our most basic principle, our *cardinal imperative: Tend to the relationship, first and always.*

It will be helpful to reconsider some fundamentals of psychotherapy in light of this relational imperative.

Acceptance

Seeking healing, the client warily allows us to enter the most tender and vulnerable regions of her soul. She will unveil things that are kept secret from the world, sometimes even from herself. She will present her daydreams and nightmares, laden with longing, shame and hope. She will explore fears, doubts, joys, desires and terrors. The risk is enormous. It is an act of heroism to make herself so dangerously vulnerable.

Our very first responsibility, then, is to provide a safe place for her to do these terrifying things. While there are practical matters to attend to in this regard (such as confidentiality and reliability), the psychological core of safety lies in the disposition of the therapist. This is largely unspoken, conveyed in subtle and subliminal ways.

The most basic requirement is *acceptance*. We often use the terms *acceptance* and *non-judging* interchangeably. The willingness to abstain from judging is indeed the first part, but it is only the negative aspect. Acceptance must also include the active verb: to reach to the other in all her idiosyncrasies, to seek her through all the pain, anger and confusion, and to embrace her being.

Some people are more difficult to embrace than others. Complete acceptance is an ideal, and we can only do our best. I think every therapist has had the experience of finding someone personally unattractive at first. Then we get to know them, to see their private wounds, defeats and struggles, to know the roots of their unpleasant presentation. We often find—sometimes to our own surprise—that we become increasingly connected with them. It's a handy rule of thumb: *When you have difficulty liking someone, look for his pain.*

Active acceptance means that I celebrate your being. I find ways to take pleasure in who you are, to enjoy being with you, even to join with you in amusement over how peculiar and funny we humans are. Playfulness, perspective and humor have a big place here.

Acceptance becomes caring. Everyone needs to be cared about, and our worst pathologies occur among people who have not had that experience. It is one of the crucial things that bring people to us.

Caring means compassion, empathy, even affection. Clients know if this is genuine. When it is not, people go away. Or, worse yet, they remain regardless of this deficit; these are the ones who don't even know that they can hope to be respected and cared about.

Caring is not easy. Caring makes us unsafe. When we care about someone we risk disappointment, anguish and loss. At the very least, we suffer their pain with them. The word *compassion* means "to feel along with."

It is understandable that we hesitate to care. It can wound us deeply. If one is unable or unwilling to suffer these wounds on a daily basis, it may be wise to consider another profession. But when we are able to care, the miracle happens: as the individual experiences acceptance and caring, he begins to accept and care for himself.

In addition, his corner of the world will be changed. Feeling accepted, he learns acceptance. There is a direct line from self-acceptance to the love of others. When we teach him to embrace everything he discovers about himself, we enable him to cherish others. When he learns to value himself and see himself as lovable, he becomes more capable of accepting and valuing others.

Technique

Technique is a basic pillar of psychotherapy. It must be neither neglected nor overvalued.

Technique is necessary for good therapy, but it is not sufficient. Salvador Dali said that one could become a good painter only after he learned to be a competent draftsman. The mere possession of pigments and brushes is not enough to create a work of art.

A good perspective on this subject was offered to me in the course of my martial arts training. The early phases of that training were focused almost entirely on technique. In the middle ranks other things were introduced: attitudes, perspectives, lessons in life which came through the practice of the art. Technique became part of a larger unity. By the higher ranks, brown and black belts, there were new realms to enter, a wisdom of motion and mind. Now there was little conscious thought of technique. It had been subsumed into a higher occupation, often referred to simply as "the way" (*do* or *Tao*).

The parallels to the student, the graduate and the experienced psychotherapist are exact. The student, and the therapist early in career, must learn technique. Otherwise he will blunder about, re-inventing the wheel and failing to learn from a rich tradition of experience. It will take him a long time to accomplish anything.

As he gains experience he will find his thoughts less often on technique. Because he is increasingly free to focus on process and content, he will quickly understand and do things that had been frustrating or difficult. Increasingly, the use of technique grows out of the relational moment.

Later, with extensive experience, the process occurs without a great deal of conscious thought. Now the practice becomes more spontaneous, more fun and more gratifying. Wisdom, confidence and the delight of relationship fill increasing portions of the day. There is still a lot of hard work and the need to endure pains and difficulties. But slowly, with experience, we earn our black belts.

Please don't be in a hurry to get there. It is the learning and the practice that provide much of the joy.

Interpretation

The psychoanalytic approach places great emphasis on interpretation, and its understandings are sometimes abstract and highly intellectualized. In our relational context, interpretation suggests understanding through connection and compassion as much as through intellect. Interpretation becomes a *relational event*, not a cognitive exercise.

To illustrate: One form of interpretation we all use is *normalization*. This is the simple and consequential act of letting someone know that we consider their behavior (or thought or emotion) to be an everyday human one; we don't see it as strange, sick or crazy. In some important way, it makes sense.

We presume that it is our knowledge or authority that convinces people to accept our benign version, and there is truth in that. But even more powerful is the interpretive event as part of the embrace of the client. It is an extraordinary validation, an act of welcome and comfort.

In the midst of a discussion of someone's eccentric behavior, my wife said to me, "You don't think *anyone* is crazy, do you?" I realized that she was right in an important way. *Everyone's thinking and behavior makes sense, if you can just get inside their frame of reference.* It makes sense to turn down a lot of money if acquiring it would violate your principles and damage your integrity. It makes sense to deliberately endure hunger if you are observing Ramadan or Yom Kippur. And it's perfectly reasonable to hide away if you truly believe that people are trying to apprehend you and send you to a penal colony on Mars. Turning down money and food, or cloistering oneself, may seem strange and counter-productive. If we understand the frame within which the ethicist, Muslim, Jew or paranoid is operating, then the things they do make sense.

In seeking an interpretation or an understanding, we can begin by assuming that this individual has good reasons for his behavior. If it doesn't make sense to us, that is not because it doesn't make sense, but because we don't yet have enough information to understand. As client and therapist seek that information together, they also strengthen their bond.

Judith has ended a series of relationships abruptly over small disappointments, sending away men she truly thought might be right for her. The panicky suspiciousness she feels at these times seems unrealistic, and she thinks there must be something wrong with her. I suggest that she must have some good reasons for her fears. As we examine her life, the roots are not difficult to see: her father vanished when she was six, and her mother had a long series of relationships ending in abuse, abandonment, or both. Then Judith saw two older sisters follow the same path. "Of course you're afraid," I say to her. "What reason would you have to trust a man? You'd be dumb not to be scared, and you're not dumb." This normalizes and humanizes the problem, allowing us a relational space in which Judith can begin to develop her choices. First with me, and then perhaps with other men, she can learn new ways to test and evaluate relationships. She can begin to manage the present rather than react to the past.

The "truth" of an interpretation is not a concrete reality like the existence of the tree in my front yard. Truth has many meanings. The way we interpret or understand something does much to determine what that reality is for us. Language, like art, does not merely describe or convey an experience of reality; it also creates that reality. When we discover a new way of perceiving something, our universe will never be quite the same. One of the therapist's most challenging and creative tasks is to see reality a little differently, and to share this vision with his client. When we change our perception of reality, we change reality itself. *Psychotherapy does not merely investigate reality; it also creates it.* When I tell Robert that his behavior with his son seems to me to be particularly tender, it may in fact become tender in his mind, whether it "really" began that way or not. This may give rise to a different vision of himself, and thus to still more kindhearted behavior.

Of course, interpretation may work in the reverse direction. Terri came to me after a long spell of therapy in another city. In our early meetings she warned me repeatedly of how "manipulative" she could be, and gave me examples from her recent life. I found the examples, as well as her behavior with me, unconvincing. I told her—truthfully—that she seemed pretty straightforward in her efforts to get what she needed from me. As we explored this difference in perception, it appeared that her previous therapist had repeatedly interpreted her behavior as manipulative, and Terri had finally adopted that view as her own. Reconsidering it now, she came to see herself as a basically honest person; as she saw herself differently, it influenced her behavior and her decisions.

The usefulness of an interpretation can best be gauged by the client's intuitive response to it. Anyone who has been in therapy has had the experience of hearing an interpretation and thinking, "Nah, that just doesn't feel right to me. It doesn't fit." While this sometimes represents resistance or denial, it is often an insightful sense about who one is, and it's arrogant on our part to insist that "She must realize that this behavior reflects the rivalry she had with her sister."

Maybe, but maybe not. We have no corner on reality. *The "truth" of an interpretation can often be reckoned only by the response of the client.* We do well to offer our ideas in the form of questions, hunches and suppositions, to be tested against the client's experience in the course of our journey.

Resistance

Today Nate brought me a dream.

When he was here last, he declares, I told him exactly what he needed to do about a difficult decision. I don't remember it that way, but that was his take and he didn't like it.

He tells me the dream he had last night. "I'm in a pool of quicksand," he relates. "It's up to my waist and I'm sinking slowly. You [meaning me, Steve] are standing next to the sand pool. You throw me a rope and it lands next to me. I don't pick it up; I'm trying to think what I want to do. You start yelling at me, telling me to grab the rope and you'll pull me out. I still don't do anything, and then you get really mad. You scream at me, dammit Nate, pick up the rope. As I sink deeper in the sand, I raise my hand, smile, and give you the finger."

The conventional idea of resistance is intrapsychic; it is something taking place within the client. For various reasons he does not want to follow suggestions, accept some unpleasant truth, or explore an important subject. But as Nate's dream tells us, resistance is not just something one brings with him to therapy. It is also relational. It is not just that "the client is being resistant." Rather, he is resistant now, with me, under these circumstances. "What does he resist?" is only half the question. The other half is "What part do I play in his resistance, and what can I do about that?"

Perhaps the client is embarrassed, fearing I will shame or judge him. Perhaps he feels pressured to do something he is not ready to do. Or maybe I'm just too bossy. I may not have won his trust. Or he could be experiencing divided allegiances: if he tells me the incident that is on his mind, he will feel disloyal to his father.

There are times we pursue a line of inquiry and the client resists examining it. Pointing out his avoidance may be enough to overcome the block, but it may not. The temptation then—one that is easy to give into—is to coax him to go ahead anyway, as the subject seems so important. This may be unwelcome; it may even be experienced as coercive. It certainly is not helpful to the sense of mutuality needed for good therapy.

Instead of pressing, we can acknowledge the hesitation: "This is difficult to talk about, isn't it?" We can offer to talk about *why* this subject is so troublesome, or to ask if there is anything we can do to make it easier. We might simply continue, "We don't have to deal with this if you're not ready. We'll get to it at the right time." With the pressure removed, the right time often comes within minutes.

We respect the resistance. It is there for a reason, and it exists between us. It is not merely in the client, but also in the relationship.

Boundaries and Limits

Paula is mad. Mad angry, not mad crazy. Well, maybe a bit of that, too.

She has stormed up to the nurses' station, demanding that she be allowed to sign herself out of the hospital. With a weary sigh, the charge nurse searches in a drawer for the proper form.

The nurse is understandably tired of this. Paula has been on the adult psychiatry service for several weeks (this was in the days when such things were possible). She goes through this performance every time she is confronted about her difficult behavior, and every time she doesn't like some restriction. The laws in this state require that the patient wait 72 hours after the discharge request is signed, so that the physician may institute commitment procedures if he or she thinks they are warranted.

Paula knows the ropes; she is aware of the 72-hour provision, and each time takes deliberate advantage of it. Somewhere between 24 and 48 hours after signing, she comes to the desk and rescinds her discharge demand. No one can recall how many times this has happened.

But one thing is different this time. In my capacity as Medical Director, I am there when Hurricane Paula arrives, and I get to witness the drama. I don't like seeing our staff people abused, and allowing this to go on is not doing Paula any good, either. So I step to the desk and address her, doing nothing to hide my irritation.

"Paula, you have a right to sign that. But if you do, you can't take it back again. You're out of here. You will have one hour to pack, get a ride home, and be gone."

I couldn't have gotten a stronger reaction if I'd hit her with a brick. She stares at me open-mouthed, and for the first time in anyone's memory she is speechless. She returns to her room. The sign-out histrionics are not repeated.

There is an interesting and gratifying sequel. A few days later Paula approaches me and asks me to become her physician and therapist. This makes sense; Dr. Childers is a sweet and well-meaning man who can't stand up to her, and they have been making little progress. She has already spoken to him about the transfer, and he has agreed.

People who are out of control desperately need to come up against limits. They may seem to be doing whatever they like, but beneath the bravado they are frequently in a state of panic. They need to know where the boundaries are. Without them no one feels safe. Those who cannot employ internal discipline— whether child or adult—need the restraints set, even imposed, by others.

Certainly Paula's dramatics were not making her any happier. I was protecting the staff by requiring her to face the consequences of her behavior, but I was also providing Paula the opportunity to gain a semblance of personal control.

This doesn't always work, but it's worth a shot. In any case, the least outcome would have been the removal of this disruptive presence for staff and other patients.

People who deal successfully with badly-behaving children are familiar with this process. Even the ordinary child having a temper tantrum needs to know that the adult will neither harm him nor let him harm himself.

Older children and teenagers have the same needs, even when they hide them (and they will!). You tell your youngster he may not go to the hockey game with his friends unless he has turned in his assignment. His school says he may not stay on the basketball team unless he maintains a certain grade-point average. You take away driving privileges for a while after he gets a speeding ticket, and make him earn the money to pay the fine. We don't expect him to like any of these consequences. He will try to make us miserable over it. But when we avoid doing these hard things, we fail our children.

In psychotherapy practice we regularly see families of adolescents who are behaving badly. Often these kids are crying out for rules and boundaries, begging to have the parameters clearly set. Kids know they need this. I have listened to teenagers *telling* their parents how the parents can make them behave better. They come straight out and say, "If you'd put your foot down, here's how I'd respond." They yearn for consistency. It's getting the parents to hear them that is often difficult.

Working in the prison system, I spoke with men whose families and communities had never taught them to think about consequences. These men complained of their treatment at the hands of others, and some of their complaints were justified. Certainly our society and our penal system can tend to callousness. But I was often amazed at how the converse side was invisible to these men; they had no consciousness that their behavior had a potent influence on how others treated them.

Good boundaries are neither rigid nor vague, neither punitive nor indulgent. When we establish and maintain such boundaries, we provide a healthy and growth-producing situation.

In seeking auspicious ways to establish guidelines in therapy, we must first set practical and ethical limits for ourselves (see Chapter 2). Then we can place reasonable and necessary restrictions on how much our clients can demand from us in time and energy, in financial credit, in availability and responsibility. Establishing these clear boundaries is good therapy, and equally important, it is good for us.

The problem of burnout is a serious professional hazard. Burnout is simply the condition of "running on empty." It occurs when we have spent too long giving out more than we get back. I find myself repeatedly addressing this issue with therapists whom I supervise. They so earnestly want to help.

Avoiding burnout requires functional boundaries, attention to our own needs, open discussion of difficulties, and even termination of therapy when that occasional client refuses to respect the person and legitimate needs of the therapist.

Therapists often have difficulty knowing the measure of their own responsibility. This is not taught in graduate school, and most of us must learn it the hard way. *One of the best means for identifying our over involvement lies in monitoring the countertransference.* We know we have taken on too much when seeing the client's name on the schedule makes us unhappy or anxious. We recognize it by our feeling of fatigue or irritability after seeing someone, or even during the session. We are over the line when we are persistently tired, when we habitually feel overextended, or when we repeatedly pass up ordinary personal activities: exercising, making time to read or see friends, taking time off.

Laura, a young psychologist, asked to join one of my supervision groups. She was bright, conscientious, warm, and tired-looking. I asked when she had last taken a vacation; it turned out that she hadn't done so in three years of practice. "I've planned vacations several times," she explained, "but someone always needs me." We made a deal: I would be her supervisor, and she agreed to schedule a vacation within six months. Further, she would not cancel that vacation without first discussing it in supervision.

When the time came, of course, someone needed her. The group alternately supported her and lovingly beat her over the head; we didn't physically put her on the plane for Jamaica, but it was close. Her boyfriend was most grateful.

I have a simple rule for myself and for those I supervise: *When you find that you are working harder than your client, you are no longer doing therapy.* When we are more invested than they are, we have fallen into the trap of caretaking, and we need to find our way out of it.

This trap is often motivated by client dependence and helplessness, along with its mirror image, therapist omnipotence. Am I offering to take charge of her life for her? Am I trying to be a miracle-worker? Do I want too much to be liked or admired? Am I feeling a lack of confidence for which I must compensate with external demonstrations of success? Am I engaged with this person therapeutically, or am I embarked on a rescue mission?

The rescue mission can alienate the very people who seem to be asking for it. I sat in with Carl Whittaker on a difficult family. Tempers were rising, and family members were turning their hostility toward Carl. He looked around at them and asked, "Why are you getting mad at me? I'm not trying to help you."

Setting limits is not easy. We may come from homes where discipline has been harsh, and loving toughness feels to us like cruelty. We may perceive ourselves as hardhearted when in fact we are only asserting the reality of consequences.

One other consideration: like every other human being, we want to be loved. That's understandable enough; but when we act on that hope we will want to do only the easy and lovable things. Our primary satisfaction must lie in the genuinely loving acts of psychotherapy, even when that requires taking a hard line. Like good parents, we cannot allow ourselves to be motivated by the hope of being loved.

Endings

The question of whether, when and how therapy comes to an end is the subject of endless debate; we find ourselves in a howling blizzard of contradictory opinions. We hear that only short-term therapy makes sense *and* that long-term therapy is necessary for real change. It is said that some therapies should go on indefinitely *and* that all must have definite endings, that termination should be a long and well-planned process *and* that it should happen the moment the work is completed. This is only a sample of the contradictions we encounter.

There are so many ways of thinking about endings precisely because clients have so many different needs, and because there are so many conflicting ideas about what therapy is to accomplish. Our notions about completion include everything from immediate symptomatic relief to probing self-understanding, from conditioned behavior change to the engendering of a "self-actualizing individual". Not only do therapists and theorists fall into many camps over these questions, but also any individual may simultaneously hold a number of different answers, as I do. Let me offer some examples.

I began working with Catherine when she was admitted to my inpatient service with crippling compulsive habits and acute persecutory delusions. Over the twenty-plus years since then, her symptoms have been largely absent or mild, but subject to occasional severe exacerbations. There have been a few brief rehospitalizations. Her ups and downs have always been connected with ongoing issues in her family of origin, most especially involving her mother's appalling rejections and criticisms. With each recurrence we have patiently unraveled the events, thoughts and feelings from which the symptoms originate. Each time we do this, she quickly recovers her balance. It is this process, along with the judicious use of medication, that has allowed her to live a fairly normal life despite her potentially paralyzing disabilities. As Catherine has stabilized in recent years, we have slowed things down; we now meet every two to four weeks, depending on need, and she has become skillful in assessing her need.

I don't foresee bringing Catherine's therapy to an end—ever. One of us will die first. Terminating therapy would be a disaster for her. There is something missing in her that will not allow that degree of stability and independence.

Mark and Beverly had been married for sixteen years; it had all been good until recently. For months now they had been fighting, and could not say what they had been fighting about. It began around the time of her father's death from cancer, yet all evidence said that she had handled that event with natural grieving.

We quickly discovered that it was her relationship with her mother that had changed. Mother had transferred her dependence from Father to Beverly, and Beverly's complicated feelings and reactions to Mother's new intrusiveness had been sabotaging her interactions with Mark. His bewildered responses hadn't helped, adding to Beverly's experience of guilt and confused loyalties.

It took only a few meetings to sort through the behaviors and feelings, enabling them to come up with new ways of seeing and handling the conflicts. They lined up on the same side of the problem, working out together what they could and could not offer her mother, and how they could set reasonable restrictions while still being supportive. The fighting stopped, replaced by a sense of working together on a shared problem. They thanked me for the help, and we ended after five sessions.

Trevor was living a life that some would call sociopathic—except that his conscience troubled him. His gambling and sexual promiscuity were not making him happy, yet he felt unable to stop. It was the threat of losing his wife and being alienated from his three children that brought him to therapy.

He stayed for four years, and the changes were extraordinary. He finally ceased paying dues to his terrifying and painful childhood, and gained a sense of his own value. That, in turn, freed him to explore the wonder of loving and being loved in his present life. These changes began in the context of our relationship, and were then carried into his connections with others.

He began to feel his work with me was ending, that he could continue his progress on his own. I agreed, and kept a careful watch on my own feelings. One of the drawbacks of the psychotherapy vocation is this: just when people are getting to be the most fun and the greatest pleasure to be with, they are ready to leave. Ending this endeavor would be a celebration for both of us, but also a loss. We took our time about it, reviewing and recapitulating, tying up loose ends, grieving and celebrating and saying our good-byes. Anything less would have failed to honor our journey together, and might even diminish some of the benefits.

A physician seeks one kind of result when attending to a diabetic patient (ongoing metabolic management), another when treating someone with appendicitis (acute surgical resolution), and a third when setting a broken bone (gradual repair). The way that any given therapy comes to an end must depend on the nature of the work, the desired and realistic results, the character of the people involved, the course and tenor of the relationship, and other factors that are rarely the same twice. *There is no formula that will substitute for thoughtfulness, flexibility and creativity. No theory can replace careful attention to the relationship.*

We hear much about "resolution" of intrapsychic issues. This includes the classical conception that healing consists of "resolving" old traumas. I've never known quite what to make of that. Certainly nothing just goes away. Our experience is always with us, always a part of us. Our physical and emotional scars do not disappear. What, then, actually happens when we leave therapy freer than we came in?

I spent the first years of my professional career working in drug rehabilitation. Our treatment center had a wonderful staff, half of us trained professionals and half of us counselors who themselves had been addicts. The combination was extraordinary, as each group learned so much from the other. Many of the counselors had been through our own program, had succeeded in other employment, and had returned to be part of the work; proud now, we had known them when they were junkies.

We referred to these folks as "ex-addicts." But after a time, perhaps three or four years, we began to notice something different. There was a quiet transformation, difficult to articulate but clearly present. Honoring this, we began refer- ring to these people as "*ex*-ex-addicts," recognizing that they were in some im- portant way different from ex-addicts.

I believe the difference was this: for the ex-addict, the struggles with drugs and addiction and the life were still entirely central to his character; as we would say today, she or he was "in recovery." After several years of living differently, some began to relocate this history and experience to a still-important but less central position in their conception of themselves. They began to move beyond recovery.

I experienced something similar as a veteran of the Vietnam War. For years after returning home, my conception of myself as a warrior was pivotal to my identity, tending at times to distort the present. Psychotherapy and other loving relationships allowed me to examine and place in context my memories, emo- tions and self-perceptions. As I did so, this blessing and curse of an identity gradually took its legitimate place among other facets of my soul; I gradually became an *ex*-veteran. The inner warrior is not gone—he will never be gone, nor would I wish him to be. But he does not have the power to affect my life that he once had. That ghost no longer haunts, and there is ample room for the rest of my spirit. The experience has not ended, has not "resolved". But it has taken its rightful place.

The idea of "closure" has become very popular, and it is reason for caution. Our experience is never closed. There is no resolution. There can be *integration*, a word related to *integrity*. To gain integrity is to achieve wholeness. What more could we ask?

CHAPTER 6
LANDMARKS

An interesting person has come to consult you. She is in possession of a vast and intricate territory, much of it uncharted. She has decided to explore it. She doesn't know how to go about that, so she seeks to hire a professional guide. That's you. Although you have not traveled this particular territory, you are an experienced explorer. You can show her how to cross the deserts, ford rivers safely, and penetrate the jungles. You have learned when to anticipate danger and how to handle the unexpected.

But it's her territory and her journey. Only she can decide where she wants to go and when she is ready to travel. Only she can know what is important to her and how energetic or curious she is willing to be. And she must be the one to decide when to travel further and when to come home.

This journey is about *her* needs. You have your own needs, your own passions and desires. You may expect satisfaction of some of those needs, including your wishes for intimate connection, intellectual and emotional challenge, and the opportunity to make a living in a meaningful way. Other desires—among them control, lust and adulation—are human and understandable, but may not be indulged on today's journey. This is one of the important reasons you engage in your own personal therapy, and have consultation and supervision always available to you.

Psychotherapy must be guided by the client's needs and desires. The therapist's are rightfully gratified only if they support—or at least don't interfere with—the client's. The therapy belongs to her. That's why *she* pays *you*.

When your agendas or goals take priority, unfortunate things happen. At worst, you will exploit the client for your own gratification, whether that involves money, sex, power or any other unconstrained motive. At the least, you will dominate the relationship or engender resistance, making her growth difficult.

The pertinence of the therapist's needs can be assessed by considering the values they embody. There have been attempts to make psychotherapy more 'scientific' by insisting that it is free of value judgments. But psychotherapy is about life, and human beings don't function in life without values and priorities. Otherwise there would be no reason to get up in the morning, or indeed to do anything.

Without values like compassion, mutuality, respect, individuality and integrity, psychotherapy becomes meaningless. If you offer me value-free therapy, I shall run the other way.

Our legitimate values as therapists are—no surprise here—binocular; they are simultaneously individual attributes and relational ones. For the individual they include autonomy, wisdom, courage and self-respect. Other values are more clearly relational: compassion, kindness, generosity and the capacity for intimacy. If, in doing therapy, I am satisfying my own desire for intimacy in a way that is respectful and non-intrusive, I am facilitating the same experience for my client. If I am gratifying my desire for power or control, I am doing so at her expense.

Returning to our exploration metaphor: orienteering consists of the set of skills by which the traveler navigates an unknown area using compass, map and landmarks. Hopefully we have drawn, in the previous chapters, a useful map for the journey. Details of that map will be different for each client, and indeed different for each day's travels. The compass consists of the therapist's own being, her carefully-tended self, experience and intuition. I hope now to offer some useful landmarks.

The four landmarks for our journey:
1. Show up.
2. Pay attention.
3. Tell the truth.
4. Don't get attached to the outcome.

I wish I could take credit for this formulation, but it isn't mine. I have tried to discover its source and found it attributed to everyone from Friedrich Nietzsche to John Lennon. It has served me well as a way to get oriented when I am confused or lost on my way. In the psychotherapy process (and in life) I frequently regain my clarity by asking which of these landmarks I have lost sight of.

Show up

Life comes without an owner's manual.

We do not "find the meaning of life." Our lives have only the meaning we impart to them through work and play, through love, through what the Buddhists call "right action." Showing up is the attempt to become conscious and to create consequence for one's life.

It is easy to opt out, to dismiss caring, to rest in the comfort of being half absent. We do that through apathy, fear, self-righteousness, habit and self-absorption. We reject meaning by clinging to custom, ideology, ignorance, intolerance and prejudice. We fail to show up when we respond to complaint or criticism with "That's just who I am," as if we have no choices. And we choose to be absent whenever we turn over to any authority the responsibility for our lives, our beliefs and our behavior.

Unconscious living is easy; becoming conscious means accepting life's labors and pains. People have always understood this, and one of our earliest stories expresses this truth. In the opening passages of the Bible, the first man and the first woman choose to "eat of the tree of the knowledge of good and bad." This is commonly interpreted as a tale of disobedience and punishment, but there are other ways to read it. To me, it speaks of the emergence of adult human consciousness.

We are told, "The two of them were naked... yet they felt no shame." Like small children, they were ignorant of embarrassment or self-consciousness. We learn that the man and the woman have been warned, "you must not eat of [the fruit], for as soon as you eat of it, you will die." The serpent—serpents in myth often represent transformation—shows the woman the tree, telling her truthfully that "God knows that as soon as you eat of it your eyes will be opened and you will be like divine beings who know good and bad." Eve sees that "the tree was desirable as a source of wisdom." Take note: the text says *wisdom*; it doesn't say *sin*. Look it up.

Seeking wisdom, she eats. Then she unselfishly gives some to the man. "Then the eyes of both of them were opened and they perceived that they were naked."

In their original state of unconscious childhood, they were innocent. They knew nothing about nakedness or shame, or about good and bad. When the man declares—after eating the fruit—that he is hiding his nakedness, God wants to know, "Who told you that you were naked?" As soon as He hears that, He knows that the humans have made their choice: they have taken on consciousness. A small child is not self-conscious. He does not know that he is naked, nor is he aware of his mortality.

I imagine this Father as being, at that moment, frustrated and proud and sad. We try to protect our children; we warn them of the dangers of the world, but they usually choose to imperil themselves anyway. He has cautioned them that growing up will expose them to responsibility and hardship, toil, pain and death. Nevertheless they have chosen consciousness, and He can no longer protect them. The possibility of paradise—unconscious and innocent childhood—is lost to them, not because they are being punished but because that's the way things are. Adam and Eve have shown up. They are now fully human.

Our first challenge is to show up.

We easily lose our way, giving in to avarice or fear, sloth or concupiscence or the love of our own cleverness. The task is to return, to show up *this time*, to commit again to choice, thoughtfulness, caring and accountability.

In psychotherapy, both patient and therapist must show up. As therapists, we must be conscious in the process. We must be willing to risk, to be challenged, to be shaken from our self-assurance and our comfortable dogmas. This can be frightening; it does not permit us to become stagnant or to fall back on easy answers. It keeps us continually vulnerable to change, even to unbidden insights. It keeps us anxious and alive.

Pay Attention

Paying attention is tricky. We see through filters of belief, emotion, language, perception and preconception. It is comfortable to see the world as we think it is, or as we wish it to be. I want to believe that the people in the next neighborhood are lazy, ignorant, ill motivated and dishonest. My people are ambitious, smart, right thinking and deserving of all that we have.

In a dominant male society, I find it convenient to believe that women are unable to think clearly, inconsequential in their agendas and in need of my guidance. It is useful to think this. I like my privilege.

Luann wants to believe that the man she is dating is good at heart, that he is changing, and that his insulting and abusive behavior won't be repeated this time. If she just loves him and does right, he will show up as the sweetheart he truly is. She is ignoring what she knows, denying it in favor of how she wishes it to be.

Another inattention occurs when I see *myself* as I wish I were. I am a selfless saint, or I am smarter and know better than everyone. And of course, in any conflict I am the wronged party and I deserve justice.

If we are to be guides for the journey, we must find ways of stepping outside of ourselves, of seeing life beyond the accustomed and the self-serving. We must ask whether the world we see is the one in front of us or the one we have been taught to see. Do we perceive ourselves truly or in fantasy? If we are to be fully present with others, we must find ways to get beyond our own horizons. There is a bonus in this: when we are able to do it, boredom and burnout are not issues. In wholly attending, we are continually stirred and renewed.

It is a matter of acceptance. Do we have the courage to accept the world, other people, and ourselves as we are? If we do, then we see more clearly. When we pay attention, we learn to withhold judgment. As we practice acceptance, our vision becomes more lucid.

Tell the Truth

Telling the truth is the essence of simplicity. But simple is not easy. Sometimes telling the truth is intensely difficult.

It may be difficult because telling the truth previously has left you vulnerable to anger, derision, punishment or abandonment. You may have learned that duplicity could ward off danger and provide safety, or that you could only be loved for the impression you made, the image you projected, the appearance of being what others wished you to be.

You may have learned to survive by hiding and lying. Deception, false appearances and camouflage became instruments for gaining safety and getting your needs met.

Telling the truth can be difficult because it means growing up and accepting the reality that we do not get everything we want. Or the even deeper truth that deceit will sometimes get us what we want, but at the expense of character, relationship and trust.

Telling the truth to and about ourselves means acknowledging that we are mortal, fallible, imperfect and ordinary. The truth is that we contain within us the same evil that we see in the world. The truth is that the inhabitants of the prisons and the asylums are much more like us than they are different, and that those who use power immorally for their own gain are enlargements and projections of our own avarice.

Confessing the truth means that we are responsible for ourselves, that we have no excuses and may not play victim. Life deals us whatever cards it chooses, and it's up to us to play them as well as we can. If we don't know how, we must find teachers; though no teacher will relieve us of our responsibilities.

The truth is that we are never wholly powerless. In the worst of situations we can still determine our own responses. In *Man's Search for Meaning*, Viktor Frankl presents the stunning vision of the individual entering the gas chamber, seemingly helpless yet still faced with the choice of how he will die, whom he will choose to be in the moment of his extinction. Will he die screaming in panic? Will he comfort those beside him? Will he fight, hoping to take a guard with him? Or embrace the children? Or pray?

The happy side is this: telling the truth sets us free—free from self-deceit, free from the fear of being discovered, free from the dark bonds of cunning. Striving to hear and speak the truth in therapy, we place ourselves under a sacred injunction. Precisely because telling the truth is difficult, insisting on it is a way of caring for our clients and for ourselves.

When we bring ourselves to speak the truth, we multiply our choices. Then we are free to be fully who we are, entirely ourselves, and connected to others in our integrity.

Don't Get Attached to the Outcome

We live in a culture that prizes results, measuring all endeavors by their endings. We are taught to gauge our lives by setting and attaining goals. Value is attached to outcome; process, quality and even ethics are easily abandoned.

This attitude is reinforced by the current economic climate of health care. The Arbiters of Everything explicitly instruct us to conduct therapy by setting "concrete and measurable behavioral goals," then doing whatever is necessary to achieve them. Other needs of the client are discounted.

Our personal inclinations may make things worse. Some of our most common errors occur when we get into the mentality of Helping People. We therapists are caretakers by nature, wanting everything to come out well for everyone. We can get deeply attached to results, to whether people are happy and whether they get what they want in life. Well-intentioned though it may be, it is a dangerous impulse to indulge.

The obsessive focus on outcome creates major problems. Setting measurable behavioral goals may give us an illusion of control and accomplishment where in fact little exists. I might prescribe an objective of "decreasing the frequency of the client's anxiety attacks," or "having the client leave the house at least once daily." These are desirable results of therapy, cursory as they are as a gauge of well being. But if we think this seriously addresses quality of life, or gives us any control over the world, we are in for a letdown.

Setting goals for another person is dangerous. When we do this to our client, we block the discovery of his own needs and directions. He will react to our agenda, unable to think clearly about his own. He will feel forced to choose between compliance and rebellion. For many people this replicates the family environment in which their own needs were dismissed as unimportant.

In any case, imposing goals is usually counterproductive. I sat one day with a group of alcoholic men in early recovery. They were talking about their spouses' attempts to manage their drinking. One man related that his wife would hand him his lunch on the way out the door each morning, accompanying this with, "Now don't drink today, dear." The group had a good laugh, for they all knew the upshot of the story.

People don't want to be told how to live their lives. Like two-year-olds, we will find ways to say, "You're not the boss of me!"

When we set goals for someone else, his legitimate needs will be sacrificed for the attainment of our arbitrarily defined result. He will be distracted from knowing and honoring the exigencies of his own life.

Focus on outcome may destroy our perception of process, skew our values, and cause us to overlook important issues. It is a short step to an "end justifies the means" mentality. Focusing too intently on making a living through my psychotherapy practice, I am tempted to make decisions for mercenary reasons alone. Attempting to reform a too-expensive medical care system, we have turned over control to people who neither understand nor care about the values and priorities of health care.

If I set the goal of getting my teenage client to stop using marijuana (perhaps at the urging of the school, court or parents), I may fail to account for the effect of his father's tirades about his worthless drug-crazed son. I may also neglect to address the parents' crumbling marriage and the fact that the boy is behaving badly to divert their attention from their incessant fighting.

Behavioral solutions sometimes work, if "work" is defined as the attainment of specific instrumental effects while overlooking other issues. A couple comes to the office with a common problem: he complains of too little sex, while she is irritated by the pressure she feels from him. That pressure, of course, diminishes whatever sexual inclination she might otherwise experience. In the days when I experimented with strategic therapy, I would have prescribed a sexual moratorium for them, setting up exercises to promote greater displays of affection while delaying erotic expectations. This would sometimes result in a decrease in the pressure she experienced, with a consequent increase in the frequency of their lovemaking. They, and I, would have checked this off as a successful outcome.

Notwithstanding, I don't do that any more. People—for good reasons of their own—find ways to resist these kinds of prescriptions. Even when they achieve the desired result, these solutions disregard the subtleties and complexities of the relationship and of each of the people in it. It misses a wonderful opportunity for them to witness and accept more of each other's uniqueness; to understand the meanings of sex and connection and desire for him and for her; and to explore a greater depth of sexual and other intimacy.

Outcome, in any case, is always uncertain. No outcome is guaranteed, nor is it ever entirely within our control. When we judge our work—or our lives—primarily by outcomes, we will be perpetually disappointed.

Lastly and again, the work we do is about relationship. Relationship is both the setting for the therapy and an integral part of the therapy itself. In so much of life, we see people destroy the rich process and complex fabric of relationship by trying to make a particular thing happen (for example, marriage). They hope rather than experience, manage rather than nurture, look for results rather than living the connection.

In the therapeutic relationship, detachment from outcome allows us to be fully joined in the present, to be animating and partnering psychotherapists instead of technicians. When we set sights on a predetermined result, we merely contrive to bring it about.

Well, then (you're asking me impatiently by now), just what *is* our job? And I answer: Our job is to join in a very special relationship, one that does not precisely exist anywhere else in life. In this relationship we combine aspects of healer, teacher, confessor, parent and friend. The relationship is built on intimacy, wisdom, instruction, astounding confidences, psychological knowledge, deep exploration and acts of love.

The therapist's responsibility is to make maximum use of herself and the therapeutic relationship, while recognizing the limitations and imperfections of life. She cannot be responsible for other people's happiness or for whether they get what they think they want. She must allow her clients to own their difficulties, and thus to own the resolutions.

Stated practically, *our task is to be with other people and to be the very best therapists we can be.* The outcome is up to God, karma and the universe.

Endnote: This material first appeared in a slightly different form in *Voices* 34,1:1998, under the title "Touchstone". Reprinted with permission. *Voices* is the journal of the American Academy of Psychotherapists. I recommend with great enthusiasm both the journal and the organization.

CHAPTER 7
DON'T JUST DO SOMETHING... SIT THERE!

Presence

Lori is going to Overeaters Anonymous, a twelve-step program. She is determined to get her cyclic eating and purging under control. She is ashamed of this problem, deriding herself—in a dreadfully stinging way—as "compulsive and impulsive". When I remark on how harsh she sounds, it resurrects her relationship with her unsympathetic and judgmental mother. By contrast, Lori felt safe with her now-deceased father, who was accepting, protective and loving with her. He was also an episodic alcoholic, but Lori has long forgiven him that. I know she still misses him.

Today she tells me something about her father that I didn't know: After a binge he would be thoroughly sick, with ataxia and vomiting. Lori would be terribly frightened that she would lose him. (As it was, he later died of other causes.)

I am struck by my association between Father's vomiting and hers. I voice the thought that throwing up could make Lori feel closer to the father who was her source of warmth and security. Lori seems not to hear me, returning to her "compulsive and impulsive" self-indictment. I wish aloud that she could stop judging herself and just attend to what she is experiencing at this moment. On the third try she hears me. I know this because she grows suddenly thoughtful, and softer. Then she becomes deeply sad. Two silent tears appear, and at the same time she feels loved and comforted. She is fully present now, and I feel tender with her. We grieve together and she is calmed. The memories of her father's love, and her sense of my present caring, are both part of this moment.

When we tend to the moment, it is eager to teach us. For Lori at this instant, it is the experience of her longing and sadness, and the safety of her father's presence. These become available to her once she is able to quiet the critical noise in her ears; that, in turn, occurs in the context of our shared presence.

For my part, it is the experience of my intuitive associations joined with my affectionate engagement with her. To be sure, this intuition is informed by my theoretical background and my clinical experience, but those are not part of my conscious thought. The association comes, laden with emotion, and I attend to it. Together, Lori and I learn something.

Listen to these people:

"I should be happy—he's perfect for me. What's wrong with me?"

"I shouldn't be scared about this."

"My mother just wants the best for me. I should be grateful."

"I shouldn't *want to* want a divorce."

Two features demand our attention. First, each speaker is resisting his or her own experience; and second, they all use some form of the word *should*. This word may set off alarms for us: when we say *should* (or *shouldn't*), it's typically someone else's idea, someone else's standard, someone else's desire for who we should be, how we should feel, what we should think. The psychoanalyst Karen Horney gave this the wonderful and self-explanatory expression, "the Tyranny of the Shoulds."

The first speaker is restless and unhappy, the second is frightened. They need to acknowledge that about themselves. The third is suspicious or resentful, and would do well to ask why she feels that way. And the fourth clearly wants a divorce; it is her frustration and fear of loss that begs attention.

Lori tells herself that she *shouldn't* throw up, and she is ashamed. When she puts that injunction aside and listens to this moment's experience, it speaks of her father and of her longing for love and safety.

Kaisha talks about the difficulty she sometimes has with eating. I ask her if she feels fat. A sophisticated professional woman of forty, a professor of history, she has been in therapy before. She smiles at what she calls my "therapeutic question" about her "body image." But I am not asking about her "body image" or trying to change how she sees herself. I am interested in her experience, in whether she feels fat. The difference in our perceptions (I find her slender and attractive) is a source of wry amusement that we share without invalidating her experience or her anxiety.

We ask people to be slow to label or explain their experience. Premature labeling and explanation can interfere with mindful appreciation. When we attend to the present moment, accepting and embracing it, not trying to alter, control or analyze it, that experience often teaches us just what we need to know.

"Here I Am"

The story is told of a young man who entered a Buddhist monastery. The next morning he approached the master timidly. "Master," he said, "I have come seeking enlightenment. Please tell me how to begin."

The master asked, "Have you had your breakfast?"

"I have," answered the student.

"Then go wash your bowl," said the master.

Moving from the Far East to the Near East, we find the Hebrew word *Hineni*. It appears repeatedly in Hebrew Scripture, and it translates, "Here I am."

In *Exodus* a voice calls a man out of the bush that burns and is not consumed. The voice calls him twice, by name, and the man answers *Hineni*, Here I am. The voice identifies itself and gives the man his mission. He is being sent to Pharaoh to demand the liberation of his people. At this moment he becomes the Prophet Moses, Leader of the Israelites, and this role will consume every moment of his long life.

Earlier, in *Genesis*, the Patriarch Abraham is called. He answers the call: *Hineni*, Here I am. He is commanded to undergo a test. He is to take his beloved son Isaac upon a mountain and sacrifice him as a burnt offering. This is a moment of ultimate terror, one that will forever haunt both Abraham and Isaac. It will also lead to the death of Abraham's wife Sarah, Isaac's mother. When we answer the call, we never know the consequences.

As a boy, the Prophet Samuel is called to his vocation. Like Moses and Abraham, he is called by name; he answers *Hineni*, and his life is forever different. This word *Hineni* conveys presence, the readiness to attend, and a (perhaps terrified) acceptance of the unknown results.

Others are summoned, not only in Hebrew Scripture but also in other traditions, and they answer with some form of *Here I am*. There is immense power in these words. They are transforming, necessarily and always. We are repeatedly addressed in our lives, but being addressed is not enough. It is meaningful only when we respond, only when we hear the call and are willing to answer. Then it has the power to affect metamorphosis, to change destiny.

This sacred metaphor holds true in our daily lives, especially in our intimate relationships. My spouse calls for my presence and I do not hear. I am preoccupied, self-absorbed, inattentive or defensive. Until I lift myself above these constraints and respond with "Here I am," her call is fruitless. My child needs my attention, understanding or support, and I don't respond. I'm too busy. At that moment I ignore the opportunity for presence, and thus for loving. But when I am able to call myself back, to say, "Here I am," a moment of creation occurs and the relationship is renewed.

Without the words "Here I am," we cannot love, cannot create, cannot effect transformation.

Melvin, protagonist of the movie *As Good as It Gets*, is confronted with a new vision. He has been an irritable and disagreeable man, hiding his obsessive crippled personality behind a mask of nastiness and insult, pretending he needs no one. Drawn out of hiding by his attraction to Carol, he begins to understand that there are other possibilities for him. In a stormy but lovely exchange, he admits to Carol, "You make me want to be a better man." Melvin elects to answer his call, to be in the present moment. He chooses transcendence and love.

The call for presence comes most often in the midst of everyday experience. Commonplace occurrences, run-of-the-mill circumstances, become the vehicle for vitality and change. In these ordinary moments our presence is requested continually. We are addressed whenever we see which right thing needs to be done. We may be called to a vocation or a mission. And we are summoned to respond whenever we understand our lives in a new way, or see the possibility of being a better person. This vision of new possibilities is the central event in most personal awakenings.

When we are willing to respond with a full heart, braving the pain and fear that may threaten, even suffering can take on new dimensions. In the first year of my training, I was assigned responsibility for a ward full of patients. We received news that Mary's husband, a man of only 51, had died suddenly of a heart attack. It fell to me to tell her. I found her in the large day room and knelt on the floor with her while she wailed. Then I saw the chaplain enter the room and head for us. I winced inside, for I expected to hear extraneous platitudes and empty comforts such as I had heard before. Mary looked up at the chaplain and asked him tearfully, "Why did this happen?" Inwardly I cringed again, but he surprised me. He knelt on the floor with us, took her hands, and said, "Mary, I don't know why. But I'm so sorry, and I grieve with you." Mary held onto him as she wept. I later hugged that man, and he and I became friends.

The willing presence of others makes it possible to endure the suffering that life can bring. When we are present for someone in pain, we offer our compassion, our "feeling along with." If you have had this experience, you know how truly sustaining it is. The words that are spoken scarcely matter. When people have been with me in the moment of my pain, I have little remembered what they have said. It is their presence I recall, and that presence has been a comfort to me. The gift of presence is not that it takes away the pain, but that it enables one to bear it.

Presence can also transform the ordinary moments. These moments call us, and we are given the opportunity to say *Hineni*, Here I am. It is our decision to respond or not to respond.

I drive my kid to her volleyball game and stay to watch. Perhaps I agreed to do so because I think I ought to, or because my wife has scolded me into doing it. I have more important things to do and I am resentful. My mind and heart are elsewhere; I am not present.

There is an alternative, if I will take it. I can choose to say, Here I am. I can decide to give myself to the moment, to connect and to care. Everything changes now. I experience astonishment and joy over this small person, amazement about who she is. The child senses my watchfulness, my presence, and she feels valued and loved. I am engaged in a silent celebration of her being, and she thrives.

The ordinary moments make up most of psychotherapy. The client expresses pain, confusion, anguish, fear or frustration. We find ourselves enveloped in atmospheres of hopelessness, despair, or incomprehensible loss. We have been trained and encouraged to think: What do I do now? How do I behave; what do I say? I know I must do something, but what?

And I remind myself, again and again: *Don't just do something. Sit there!*

Doing something is easy. If we can't think of things, hundreds of authors are prepared to tell us what to do. Say this! Interpret that! Direct the client to... (One book even instructs the therapist when to smile!). It is being fully in the moment, unconditionally *with* this person, that is difficult—and healing.

When I enter the moment, allowing behavior and demeanor to emerge from my attentive presence, everything alters. Old ways of seeing begin to change. I perceive myself differently, and my place in the world seems larger. I am connected and responsive. What seemed a burden can now become an occasion for meaning and fullness.

When we respond by saying "Here I am," there is no going back. We enter a new way of being in the world and a new awareness of ourselves. We are touched in our being.

Presence is here and now. We cannot alter the past; the future is unpredictable and beyond control. In this moment—and only in this moment—we are in control of our being. This is the instant of choosing, the timeless juncture in which we decide whether or not to destroy, exploit, or spin the web of deceit. This is the instant in which we can give meaning to the past or transform the future. In this singular, luminous moment we choose presence or absence, love or indifference, good or evil.

Presence is here and now; it does not keep time. When we are fully in the present there is no time. We are not immortal, but we are—in this instant—eternal and timeless. We are here, now, in this moment and nowhere else. We walk, we breathe, we see and hear. We are no one but who we are, doing nothing but what we are doing. There is only the present, only now, and now is all of time.

Distractions

> "We've come to wish you a Very Happy Thursday," said Pooh.
> "Why, what's going to happen on Thursday?" asked Rabbit, and when Pooh had explained, and Rabbit, whose life was made up of Important Things, said, "Oh, I thought you'd really come about something," they sat down for a little. . . and by-and-by Pooh and Piglet went on again. The wind was behind them now, so they didn't have to shout.
> "Rabbit's clever," said Pooh thoughtfully.
> "Yes," said Piglet, "Rabbit's clever."
> "And he has Brain."
> "Yes," said Piglet, "Rabbit has Brain."
> There was a long silence.
> "I suppose," said Pooh, "that that's why he never understands anything."
> A.A. Milne, *Winnie the Pooh*

That great sage, Winnie the Pooh, tells us about Rabbit's Cleverness and Brain. Important Things so preoccupy Rabbit that he doesn't understand that Pooh and Piglet simply want to be with him. His mind is on Things and he doesn't get it that they love him. The Rabbit Mind in each of us prevents us from hearing our call. It deafens us to the opportunities for presence and tenderness that reach out to us at each moment.

We are more hurried all the time, often overwhelmed by everyday necessities. Lois is a nurse in a urologist's office. The doctor specializes in the treatment of erectile difficulties, and over the years Lois has taken hundreds of detailed sexual histories. She tells me that even married couples are having sex less often than they did ten years ago. When you are too busy to make love with your mate, you are *too busy*. This speaks to a frightening lack of relational presence in our culture.

Time, energy, and physical resources are finite. These constraints place limits on our presence. But when we practice being present, it creates more of the same within us and in others. The uncomplicated act of your being present with me invites me to be present with you, and with myself. Thus begins a cycle of relational bounty instead of poverty. Being fully present opens us to connection, understanding and kindness.

Making the Gods Laugh

The fashion for "goal-directed therapy" has become increasingly popular. Our desires for order, control and economy make this approach most appealing. But setting goals gives us an illusion of control where in fact little control exists.

I have worked in emergency and trauma units. I have seen how catastrophically life can change in a single breath, in ways no one could have anticipated – the sudden ruin of function, the broken spine that leaves one paralyzed, the dreadful loss of a child for whom the parent was making plans only that morning. These are extreme examples; smaller instances fill each day. This is how the world works, without regard for our yearnings or desires. Life is what happens to you while you are making other arrangements. A Greek folk adage prompts us: If you want to make the gods laugh, tell them your plans.

Forcing goals on others is both disrespectful and dangerous. When I do this to my patient I get in the way of her need; I block the trail to the discovery of her own directions. She will react for or against my agenda, barely able to consider her own. She will be confounded by the obstacles I have erected, distracted from knowing and honoring her needs and the direction of her own energies.

In my senior year of college I was unexpectedly offered a graduate assistantship in philosophy, a subject I loved (and still do). Having already been accepted to medical school, I faced a dilemma. I turned to my parents for counsel. My father, a volatile man, went off the charts. He had been deeply invested in seeing me become a physician, and the prospect of a change at this point was more than he could bear. He angrily and relentlessly pressured me to come to the "correct" decision. I returned to school not only undecided, but also baffled about how to make a decision. Whichever option I chose, how would I know it was mine? How could I tell if I was submitting to my father's will if I chose medical school, or merely rebelling against him if I didn't?

Confused and unnerved, I sought out the professor who had recommended me for the assistantship. He declined to support any particular resolution; instead he invited me to join him the next day for a hike in the Central Pennsylvania mountains. There he shared with me some of his own life (his father had been a physician who had hoped his son would follow) and helped me separate my desires from my father's. His unreserved presence, entirely goal-less, paved the way for me not only to make a decision, but also to claim it as my own. What more could he have done for me? What more can we do for our clients?

The willingness to be uncommitted to an outcome allows us to be generous parents, teachers, friends or therapists. When we set sights on a desired result, we merely contrive to make it happen. When we give up striving for goals and objectives, we wander through new and delightfully uncertain lands, nourishing ourselves on the excitement of discovery and the wonder of the moment.

CHAPTER 8
PITFALLS

Psychotherapy is ultimately about how we influence our clients and are influenced by them. It is a guided interaction of personalities, producing change in both. We employ all sorts of techniques, maneuvers and procedures. We try to describe and even to prescribe behavior that we think will lead to healing. In the end, the real power of therapy resides in who we are in the relationship. Nothing else will do.

Once again, the person of the therapist is the decisive element. In the most radical and fundamental sense, the therapy depends on who we are when we are with our clients.

The key pitfall, then, is the failure to lay claim to who we genuinely are. In one way or another, it always comes back to that.

Traps and Pitfalls: It's About Us!

Vicki is drop-dead gorgeous. The sort of tall, leggy gorgeous that adolescent boys dream about. Um, well, middle-aged men, too.

She's also a very good person, and I've enjoyed working with her. In the several years we have been together she has gone a long way toward getting over her sexually abusive father, and learning to like and respect herself. As one result, she ended a long-standing destructive romantic relationship. Her life is going well now.

A few evenings ago she was having a drink with a friend when a well-dressed man asked to join them. After a little chatter, he disclosed that he runs a club for business execs, and is looking for a few more exotic dancers. Vicki says the money is terrific, and the idea excites her in an odd way that she doesn't understand. What do I think?

I think I'm responding with my hormones. Therapeutically I'm useless. I have an embryonic fantasy of watching Vicki dance naked, but I don't allow myself to go there. Actually I don't go much of anywhere, and I'm not being very helpful to her. I'm too busy trying to observe the Prime Rule: Do No Harm.

The people in my peer supervision group are most supportive. They appreciate my testosterone madness and help me to laugh at myself. Perspective restored, and feeling again more paternal than libidinous, I am able to guide Vicki in sorting out what this is about for her: the simultaneous fascination and repulsion of exposing herself again to what would be—for her—a sexually abusive situation.

•

I don't know why Abbey and I are fighting like this.

She has made slow progress over several years. There are deep and stubborn character issues here, and they yield only gradually; relearning is difficult. To use a bit of shorthand, she was diagnosed by her previous therapist with "Borderline Personality Disorder." That's not a term I like much (more of that in Chapter 9), but it will give you some idea of her difficulties in relationships. Despite that, I care for her and I'm invested in her well being.

Yet we are clashing. Even with some ups and downs, this conflict has not characterized our relationship; it is recent. But I find myself getting so upset with her now. What's going on?

What's going on is that Abbey is moving to another part of the country in two months. That means a termination of our therapy, ready or not. I am referring her to Karen, an excellent therapist whom I know, so she will be in good hands.

But I want her to be stronger and on safer ground before she goes. I see now that I have been pressing her to be "ready," trying to push her beyond where she really is. She, rightfully, has been resisting these efforts, and I have been acting out of frustration.

I am doing this out of concern for her, right? Well, yes, but further introspection reveals that there's more. I also want Karen, a valued friend of mine, to see how well I have done with Abbey. I want her to think good things about me and my work.

I decide to keep to myself the part about Karen and my ego, but I share the rest with Abbey, and I apologize for getting in her way. My confession clears the air and we proceed over the next two months to a much better ending.

•

Once we get beyond a certain level of inexperience, most of the mistakes are about us, not about our clients or about any special knowledge that we lack. With Vicki I fell prey to my erotic imagination; with Abbey, it was genuine concern plus ego. Much of the therapy is about who we are when we are with these folks, so it only makes sense that the problems frequently lie within us. It is, again, why supervision and personal therapy are invaluable.

Let's consider some of the common ways that we create our own stumbling blocks. The most experienced among us are not immune. I am familiar with these mistakes because, as you can see, I have made every one of them. A lot.

Taking responsibility for the client's life. Some people are naturally adept at sensing the moods and relational tones of others. If we look at the family histories of therapists, so many of us—at a remarkably early age—perceived discord in the people around us and thought it was our job to do something about it. We may still be trying—now by proxy—to accomplish that task.

Assuming this responsibility impels us to rescue people rather than allowing them to manage the pains and triumphs of their own lives. It occurs whenever we protect them from the conflicts of relationships and the difficulties of mortal existence. We mean well, but the results are not respectful. No one grows. My 24-year-old client is stuck in adolescence precisely because his father tries so hard to assure that he never suffers consequences.

Our task is not to rescue or protect people. Our task is to provide the relational environment in which they can undertake the unearthing of their own destinies.

Being sacrificial. Debbie gave up a nursing career to become a therapist, partly so she wouldn't have such punishing work hours. It isn't happening that way.

Her practice has taken off, and her days keep growing longer. She looks drained, her friendships are suffering, and her family misses her.

She is startled when I suggest that she turn away new referrals—after all, these are people in need. She has always thought it her duty to respond to everyone's requests, to answer every call. It is a new notion that the requirements of her own life must sometimes take precedence.

When we do not care for ourselves, we quickly become depleted. What we give will turn increasingly unproductive and barren. To damage ourselves in this way is no favor to the people who turn to us. Time, energy, money, personal privacy—all must be rationed, for our resources are not boundless. Those who try to save the whole world end up being punished by it.

Relying on the rules. There must be congruence between what we do and who we are. The rules can only provide guidelines. They cannot tell us what is healing at this moment, and they cannot account for the quality of each relationship and the personalities of each therapist and client. The rules cannot make allowance for individual temperament or experience. If we only practice "by the book," there will be many people whom we cannot help. Rigid adherence to rules and to prescribed techniques discourages personal connection; without that connection there will be little real healing.

On the other hand, it is foolish to ignore the formal systems of ethics and practice, standards set by our professional boards and civic governments. Standards are necessary to protect both profession and public, yet they carry an inherent dilemma: these standards are not exclusively concerned with ethics. They also have legal and political purposes that may or may not be congruent with the client's welfare.

Strict adherence to rules encourages rigidity, and rigidity precludes the personal. No system of rules can promote the qualities of judgment and compassion, or the balancing of complex priorities. *Unthinking observation of ethical rules can actually lead us to unethical behavior.* More of this in our closing chapter.

Several traditions tell us never to touch a patient, or perhaps to allow only a formal handshake. For some clients this restraint is appropriate and even necessary; for others, a touch or a hug at the right moment creates connection and hope. Observing a rule without accounting for the needs of *this* individual, or the requirements of *this* relationship, leaves us with arbitrary restraints and a weakened bond.

Being "objective." This is a close cousin to relying on technique. *Objective* is the converse of *personal*. It signifies dealing with *objects* rather than *people*, and psychotherapy is about people. Being objective would entail keeping our feelings, intuitions, and even our genuine concern out of the work. It pretends to a degree of disinterest that we hope never to achieve.

Knowing best. We think we know what others should do. I know that Tommy should leave his parents' home and go to college. I see that Theresa will be better off if she ends her marriage. And it is obvious that Jack should stop drinking.

But they all resist my solutions. Tommy needs more maturing before he is ready to leave, and will be much happier going to trade school rather than an academic institution. For Theresa, staying in her marriage is her best available way of taking care of her two children. And Jack's wife has been nagging him for years; he would experience abstinence as a humiliating capitulation.

Why would I think I know what is best for these folks? I'm just not that smart. It's difficult enough to know what's best for me in a particular situation. How would I know for someone else?

We all resist being told what to do, how to live, and who to be. *If we want to give folks room to change, we begin by accepting who they already are.*

Hiding behind the transference. Carol is upset with me. Last time she was here she spoke of her concerns about her elderly mother. My response was off the mark, and she felt I wasn't hearing her.

So I interpret this: her mother does not listen to her, which has always been a source of great frustration. She doesn't expect to be heard, so she projected it onto me and thought I wasn't listening.

Wrong response, dummy! It makes her even angrier. I blew it; I was too solicitous of my own ego, and didn't want to admit my blunder. It's the therapist, stupid!

Carol deserves better. The fact is that I was distracted and I *didn't* do a good job. It happens.

Since I'm writing this story, I get to go back in time and do it over (how we wish life were like that!). This time I tell her, "Carol, I'm sorry. I got sidetracked and didn't listen very well. Of course you were annoyed. But I'm here now, and I'm all ears. Would you tell me again?" She does, and we get on with our work. A few minutes later I have the opportunity to comment on the irony that she was complaining about how her mother doesn't listen, and at that moment I wasn't listening.

There is an experiential relationship and a transference relationship, and at this moment they exist side-by-side. I made a mistake, and it would be better not to hide behind the transference. Oops.

On the other hand, there is...

Grandiosity, or: Not crediting the transference. I was reviewing my work with Dr Rogers, a wonderful training supervisor. I told him about an attractive female client who had been coming on to me, and I said, "You know, that's been happening to me a lot." He dryly commented that perhaps that's because I was so terribly irresistible. His sarcasm wasn't lost on me. He smiled benignly and said, "Don't flatter yourself. It's transference. They still do it with me, and I'm 74 years old."

Clients will attribute all sorts of wonderful (and occasionally terrible) qualities to us, out of their own desires, fears and distortions. It is so easy to allow ourselves to be seduced.

Ignoring countertransference and other feelings that arise within us. I've said it and I'll repeat it: we *will* have a full spectrum of feelings about our clients. This is inevitable. This is human. To pretend otherwise is to delude ourselves.

The danger lies not in these emotions and impulses, but in our reluctance to be mindful of them. Lack of consciousness denies us important information and allows us to act on temptation and impulse. If we are to avoid responding blindly and causing harm, these affects must be acknowledged.

Recognizing temptation is not always easy. Question: When you hear that voice calling you to do something, how do you know whether it comes from God or the devil?

Answer: The devil tells you to do what you already want to do.

When I find myself having difficulty with someone's therapy, it is most often because I haven't identified my own attitudes and reactions. Dealing with these influences is by far the most valuable part of consultation and supervision.

These feelings *will* occur. Count on it. The essential question is whether we recognize them, manage them, and use them in the service of the client's therapy.

Promoting dependence. It is gratifying to have people depend on us. It tells us that we are useful, powerful and important.

This is not a bad thing. People come to us in need, and a degree of dependence is often part of the process.

No one thinks it is a problem when the heart patient is dependent on his cardiologist. And as with cardiac patients, there are some people who must continue to rely on us. They simply don't yet have the resources to become entirely independent; a few people may never have that capability. An example of this latter is described in the section on Endings in Chapter 5.

In most cases people learn and develop, and at some point begin to outgrow their dependence on us. As with childrearing, it is our job to encourage and assist this process. We must do this even though it incurs a loss for us. If we stand in the way because of our own need, or simply through a fondness for the client and a desire to continue seeing him, unhappy outcomes are likely. He may become needlessly dependent, remaining in a semblance of psychotherapy long past his time. Conversely, he may become rebellious, leaving therapy in ways that are detrimental and sometimes hostile. This is not what we are here for.

Therapist Transparency

The question of therapist transparency, also spoken of as disclosure, openness or revelation, has been controversial from the beginning of psychotherapy. Do we reveal ourselves to our clients? If so, how? How much should they know about us, and in what ways? What connection is there between our behavior as therapists and the ways in which we live our lives?

Our position on these questions will be deeply influenced by our understanding of the dynamics of psychological healing. The image of the impersonal, non-revealing therapist owes much to classical psychoanalytic thought. In this view, therapeutic healing occurs as one "works through transference distortions." The client develops attachments (transferences) to the therapist based on introjections and projections from his experiences with childhood figures, especially with parents. These associations are interpreted by the therapist, who, in order to encourage the development of this transference, remains a detached, non-disclosing "blank screen." As the client gains insight into his unconscious dynamics, he can correct these distortions and "undo his neurosis." Presumably, when all these psychic deformities are corrected, he is well. As best I understand it, this is what constitutes the "well-analyzed" individual.

Many analysts and psychodynamic therapists since Freud have modified these ideas, and some have begun to incorporate the project of relationship. Object-relations theory and attachment theory both furnish examples of this welcome revisionism.

Looking at psychotherapy from our relational perspective leads us to some different conclusions, having more to do with our humanity and fallibility.

It is easy to think that we must be, or at least appear to be, perfect.

"How can I do therapy with couples when my own marriage is still so difficult?"

"What if a client sees me at my AA meeting and knows that I've struggled with a drinking problem?"

"I got into a fight with my kid at the mall, and just then my client came up and heard it. I'm so embarrassed!"

Back in the real world, it's fortunate that we needn't have everything right in our own lives in order to be helpful to others. If being therapists meant that we had to have it all together, there would be no therapists.

If we are willing to be seen as human and imperfect, we offer our clients an attitude that says, "You and I are not very different. We all struggle; we all have to deal with our pain and fear. We all have shortcomings and flaws and just plain foolishness. I've learned a bit about how to make that work in life, and you can, too. If you think I'm a good example for you, know that I wasn't born this way. I worked hard to get here, and I had help." The client needs to understand that we make mistakes, that we struggle in our own lives, and that we can be inconsistent and even ridiculous. The therapist's appearance of being flawless, beyond struggle and anguish, can send a message of hopelessness; the client thinks, "I can never expect to be like that, so I am condemned to suffer." When he sees us accepting our foibles and eccentricities with humor and a sense of irony, he learns to sound the same grace notes for himself.

The notion of the objective, impersonal therapist is problematic for another reason: it is an illusion. On the most practical level, anonymity (literally, the state of having no name) is often unrealistic. We may live in the same community as our clients, encountering them at the supermarket, movie theater, church or symphony. They may hear of us by reputation. They might know our spouses or children, and we can easily have friends in common. I have had people come to me because they resonated with something I had written, often something with a highly personal flavor. And some of my clients are therapists whom I see at professional meetings or who attend my educational workshops.

In any case, much about us is evident regardless of what we do. The therapy office is in a certain location and is decorated in a way that speaks of who we are. They see the artwork and the furniture we have chosen, and they may know our office mates. The values by which we live and practice are easily discernible after even short acquaintance. We show ourselves by the subjects in which we are interested, and in our reactions and responses to the things we hear. Even when we think we are not revealing ourselves, we disclose a great deal in our gestures, postures, vocabulary, tone of voice and facial expressions.

A variant of this anonymity theme is embodied in the idea that we can be "non-directive." Certainly we can and should refrain from telling people how to live their lives. But we indicate direction every time we ask a question, pursue a line of thought, or display an interest in something that is said. I have never remembered more than an occasional dream of mine, but when I was in therapy with someone who exhibited a strong interest in dream interpretation, I produced vivid and memorable images every night. He did not instruct me to do this; I was responding to his show of interest.

Transference remains important, and we have considered these issues earlier. While transference work is only one of a number of healing factors, the identification of transference distortions can be a vital step in a powerful reorientation. However, it needs to be explicitly stated that *the identification of transference is not curative*. Rather, it is the first step in a larger process.

Put briefly, classical theory portrays the transference work as occurring exclusively in the client's mind; the therapist simply offers interpretations. But transference healing is a binocular event. It occurs within the individual *and* as an aspect of the relationship.

Philip habitually thinks the worst of himself. We come to understand that the critical voice in his mind had its genesis in his desire to please his faultfinding and unaccepting father. As often happens, he expects the same judgments from me.

He is a smart guy, and intellectually he knows better. But in matters emotional, smart is no match for experience. We expect to be treated as we have always been treated.

Yet, we continue to hope. Cautiously at first, Philip tests this new relationship, revealing increasingly sensitive areas, expecting reproach, rejection or punishment. It is breathtaking when, instead, he is met with understanding and even tenderness. So he risks more, goes deeper, reveals his bruised insides. At each step he anticipates the worst.

Now he finds himself with a mystifying double vision. He sees in me the image of his father, and simultaneously he sees me, the person he is coming to know in the present. His vision of me is not a "neutral" one; it isn't simply that he is not being judged. At most, that would amount to a passive lack of harm, perhaps even indifference. If you have ever been loved by a dog, you know that the dog's lack of criticism is only the beginning. His overwhelming, joyful and irresistible presence tells you that he celebrates your existence with every fiber of his body. We have much to learn from our dogs about the expression of love.

Philip's double vision of me becomes a double vision of himself. Like any diploplia, this one is dizzying, even disorienting. Out of one eye he sees his old, habitual image: I am not loved because I am not lovable. With the other eye he discovers a different image, one that announces to him: "This person is glad for my presence. He connects with me without reservation. He thinks that I am good and acceptable and—dare I think it?—lovable."

Wary at first, then astonished, he comes to recognize that he is indeed considered worthwhile, even lovable. He is lovable not because he meets some standard of mine, and not because of what he can do for me, but because I think he is deserving in himself.

The experience of holding these two contrasting visions at the same time affords the opportunity for new learning about oneself. There is no deeper kind of healing.

The power of the therapist's acceptance does not reside only in the transference, even though it may begin there. In the end, *the regenerative acceptance and compassion can come only from an authentic human being who is willing to care in a connected and personal way.*

This is a relationship, and a relationship is an interchange. Carl Jung wrote, "The meeting of two personalities is like the contact of two chemical substances: if there is any reaction, both are transformed." To pretend that we are less than whole people is to do a disservice to ourselves and to our clients.

None of this should be taken to imply a wild and unfiltered openness, or a surrender of our own privacy and integrity. I am speaking of personal presence, honesty and vulnerability, not of forced exposure. It is important that we be real people, not that we tell about our lives; the latter can sometimes get in the client's way. How much we choose to tell will depend on many things: our comfort level, the client's comfort level, the duration and nature of the particular relationship, the relevance to the client's situation, and so forth. When my client is grieving a loss, it may be helpful to hear about some of my feelings when my father died, even to see my sadness and loss; but I must not use his time to do my own essential grief work. Nor is it always wise to speak everything you are thinking about the client; you may be wrong, or he may not be ready to hear it, or the context may be misleading. Honesty does not mean total transparency, nor does it justify a lack of judgment and critical thinking.

We have all had clients comment that they know little of us while we know so much about them. They may say, "I don't know who you are." But personal presence doesn't always mean telling. It means being. We might properly respond, "You may not know a lot about the facts of my life, but you know a great deal about who I am."

PART TWO

JOURNEY MAPS

CHAPTER 9
CLASSICAL CONSIDERATIONS

Psychological Theory

The first agenda in therapy is, of course, beginning an alliance. The second is establishing a preliminary understanding of the client and her distress, and of what brings her to our offices now rather than at some other time. Thus begins a trail map for the journey.

The need for understanding has given rise to numerous theories of personality that attempt to make sense of who we are and how we function. They also offer us ideas about what is right (healthy) and wrong (unhealthy or broken) about us.

The more we study these theories—and I have studied them, even taught them—the more problems we encounter. The first is that there are so many different ideas and formulations. A good rule of thumb: when we have a lot of theories to explain something, it's because we don't have one really good one.

The second problem lies in the very nature of theory. A theory should not be mistaken for reality. A theory is an idea, a conceptual handle by which we can think about reality and perhaps manipulate it. It is the best current explanation for the observed facts. In scientific inquiry, a theory is established only after arduous scrutiny and testing to determine whether it fits—and then predicts—observable data. When I claim that human beings are relational creatures, you can test that against all your experience of people. If my formulation fits your observations in a way that is useful, it is a pretty good theory. If the explanation is inadequate for the facts, then we need to modify, add to, or get rid of the theory. No theory is "really true", just more or less adequate as an explanation.

Thirdly, we have developed many of our ideas about psychological health through observation of people who are in pain or who are not functioning well. This is much like trying to understand lung physiology by examining people with pneumonia and tuberculosis. We have an intuitive grasp of physical health; if we can't define it, we at least think we know it when we see it. Our ideas about psychic health are more nebulous, and too frequently ideological (religious, cultural, psychological, social). It seems to me that questions of optimal human living fall in the domains of philosophy and theology as much as those of psychology or medicine.

Most of our theories explore the individual psyche; certainly the psychodynamic ones do. But we are maintaining that the individual does not exist in isolation. He is the focal point of a rich and complex set of relationships; he exists in them like a fish lives in water. We cannot truly appreciate the lives of human beings without accounting for the fabric of our relationships.

However intricate and imaginative a theory may be, people are even more complex. There is a great deal that theory simply will not account for. Life is overwhelmingly ambiguous and multidimensional, full of irreducible mysteries; among them love, death, childbirth and awe.

The final problem with theory is its imperfect relevance to daily clinical practice. Listening to therapists talk about what they do is often very different from watching them do it. If we watch recorded sessions of relatively new practitioners, it is easy to discern the approaches in which they have been trained. When the therapists are more experienced, it can be a challenge to determine their theoretical and operational backgrounds; we distinguish them more by their personal styles. Experienced therapists have learned what works for them, and, unsurprisingly, they keep doing it.

Given all these objections and caveats, theory is very much worthy of study. Any genuinely thoughtful formulation is likely to conceptualize *some* aspects of reality. While no theory will approach the rich complexity of real people living real lives, each can yield some helpful understanding. In an exam I gave to my graduate students in theory class, I related a real-life case history and asked them to describe the situation from the point of view of several of the theories we had studied—Jungian, Object Relations, Bowinian, and so forth. The answers were creative and interesting, and demonstrated that there was no theory that couldn't be put to some use. The problems arise when we insist that the theories represent truth itself.

A theory is a stepping stone; it enables us to cross the stream and wind up on the other side. It's not much of a journey that leaves you standing on the stone in mid-stream.

Diagnosis in the Real World

"What's my diagnosis?" Eddie asks me toward the end of his therapy. He himself is a therapist.

Eddie and I have worked together for four years. We have begun wrapping up, and his question must be taken seriously (but not, I hope, too seriously). I give it some thought.

"Let's see, Eddie. We know that you're an anxious person. One solution for that anxiety was drug abuse; you don't do that anymore. The other is with the women in your life. We've seen how you are interested in someone, or just have sex with someone, and you're suddenly *in love*. That usually translates as feeling hopelessly dependent. You've described it yourself, how you feel as though your umbilical cord runs through your penis and you plug into her to be nurtured.

"In the last year or two you've been learning that you don't have to do that, that finding the right woman is not going to be your salvation. You've started accepting that you're just going to have to work at life, and it will never give you the perfection we all long for."

Eddie thinks this over. Then he says, "O.K., I get that. But what's my diagnosis?"

"Eddie, that *is* your diagnosis."

The word stems from the Greek root *gnosis*, referring to knowledge. To *diagnose* is to understand. My diagnosis of Eddie is an attempt to encapsulate some useful knowledge about his life.

Every profession and trade has its own jargon, and diagnostic terms are part of ours. Jargon serves two important functions. It can be a way of saying a great deal in a few words; rather than spend several sentences describing someone's mental processes, you will understand my meaning when I use words such as "transference" or "dissociation".

Jargon is also a way of being exact. If I tell you that someone is being passive-aggressive, I have conveyed certain behaviors and dispositions with a fair amount of precision. When technical terms do not serve one of these two functions, condensation or precision, we are better off expressing ourselves in ordinary language. Otherwise, jargon complicates and obfuscates. At best, like puffing on a pipe, it makes us seem wise when we really just need time to think.

Diagnosis has its uses, and also its dangers. Its first snare is the illusion that a diagnosis is a reality. In truth, a diagnosis is a construct, a myth or metaphor for something we wish to describe. Like a theory, a diagnosis is helpful only if it allows us to conceptualize and express an idea. To say that Eddie has a "dependent personality disorder" turns a set of tendencies into an inexact label that gives us little to work with. It sounds like something we must excise from Eddie, like a tumor. It certainly doesn't relate to his lived experience or to my rich and intimate dialogue with him.

The other danger is the tendency to see a diagnosis as defining a person. I recall my astonishment when a physician on rounds referred to his patient as "the gall bladder in room 233". If the patient isn't a gall bladder, neither is she a schizophrenic, a borderline, or an obsessive-compulsive. These terms can be useful when they describe an individual's ways of relating to the world, to other people, and to herself. They have no independent reality. Diagnosis is not identity.

Let us return to our binocular perspective. We would do well to understand diagnostic thinking as expressing something not only about the individual, but also about the individual *in relationship*. My description of Eddie expresses something of what he does both internally and relationally.

During an evaluative session, I might write, "The client shows flat affect throughout the interview". This sounds like an objective quality, like the color of her eyes; my presence on the scene is only that of an observer. But the reality is that the subject is showing flat affect *in this conversation with me*. Probably this is a habitual defense when she is feeling threatened, and thus it is information about this person. But her experience of feeling threatened is happening now and with me. If I garner the patience and skill to relieve her sense of danger, I will probably see her come alive.

A teen-age boy is diagnosed with Oppositional Disorder. It sounds like opposition is an illness, an inflammation somewhere in his body. But I know his overbearing family, and it makes sense that he is defiant; in his perception, his very integrity is at stake. Change what happens in the environment and his "disorder" may disappear.

This raises a fundamental question: what is a "disorder" anyway? Our use of the word implies that, like Aristotle, we know what a proper "order" is. Do we? Can anyone tell me exactly what a "functional" family looks like? Such terms are normative, embodying our own personal and cultural ideas about what is "natural" and "healthy". It was not long ago that homosexuality was listed as a pathology.

A few other thoughts on the issue of diagnosis:

We can fall into the trap of using diagnosis as an expression of our anger, distaste or helplessness. "Borderline Personality Disorder" may be the worst offender. The term can be used with precision to describe certain ways of experiencing and relating, but more often than not I hear it used as a pejorative: "Well, what can you expect? She's a borderline." In other words: I don't know how to deal with her; she frustrates me and I don't like her. We do well to use diagnostic terms relationally and descriptively, not allowing them to represent our judgments of people and our difficult feelings about them.

Diagnosis runs in fads and styles. A few years ago we heard a great deal about "co-dependence". To my great relief, I seldom hear this ill-defined term today. Multiple Personality was wildly popular for a while, to the point where hospitals were opening entire units for this rare problem. Early editions of the Diagnostic and Statistical Manual were full of different "neuroses", another term we thankfully no longer use. How many of today's "disorders" will be missing from future editions?

Diagnosis may also be personal to the clinician. I was doing some psychological research at a large mental health hospital, testing patients on different wards. Looking at the diagnoses on the charts, I saw that one unit was filled with schizophrenic people, another with patients with various personality disorders, and a third with borderlines. When I inquired how people were distributed in this way, it turned out that placement on units was random, determined by the availability of beds. However, each ward had a different resident physician, and each resident had a favorite diagnostic category.

Diagnosis may be situational. If you try to have a conversation with Linda today, you will find her to be anxious, unfocused, a bit incoherent, and at times "spaced out", seemingly in poor contact with those about her. A number of diagnoses suggest themselves. It turns out that she is having a brain scan today to investigate the possibility of a tumor, and her anxiety is overwhelming. On another day you would encounter a very different person.

Finally, we are dealing with complex and inconsistent human beings. Personalities, traits and ways of relating cover huge spectra, and we should be cautious about our perceptions of pathology. Obsessive and compulsive traits, for example, can be troublesome and even crippling. But they can also be highly adaptive: I want my airline pilot, my accountant and my surgeon to be very, very compulsive, thank you.

About "Crazy"

People will try to define us, often for their own comfort. They will even attempt to limit what we think and who we can be. Under the pressure of these demands, we can become trapped in the confines of our lives, no longer knowing how to be true to ourselves; spiritually, we are dying. At such times it may be that only an act of desperation provides an escape from this lethal prison.

In everyday speech we call these acts of desperation "nervous breakdowns". The phrase has no scientific or medical definition, but it may have a deep personal significance. Breakdowns take many forms, but they all consist of frenzied behaviors that *break down* the walls that trap us. It looks strange and frightening, and people are likely to see it as illness, disaster or moral failing. The breakdown creates chaos and threatens unpredictable change. It can also be a time of great opportunity, for the crisis carries the possibility of new vitality and freedom. The nervous breakdown is our way of telling ourselves and everyone else that something *must* be different. It is a jail break.

Mimi was living in desperation so quiet that even she did not realize she was coming apart inside. Single until age thirty-three, she had enjoyed what she called "the butterfly life". Having decided on marriage, she was determined to be a good and faithful wife. Her model for this was her parents' loving but very traditional and role-bound relationship. She coerced herself into this pattern without regard for her own temperament, and she tried to incorporate her husband Tom's pre-feminist ideas about what a wife should be. In doing so, she entombed the playful, unconventional and sensual free spirit she had been when she was single.

Tom came home one day to find her sitting on the sofa looking decidedly strange. Two of her fellow teachers had brought her home from school. Her speech was rapid, jumbled and confused, and she was intermittently delusional and disoriented. She had moments of lucidity and even humor; in one of them she said with a twinkle, "I thought for a few minutes I was Hillary Clinton—and I don't even like Hillary Clinton."

The confines were tumbling like walls in an earthquake. Frightening as it was, she could no longer live inside her self-imposed prison. She was seeking escape by doing the only thing she could find to do—lashing out wildly and breaking down everything about her. In these situations, our profession sometimes does a terrible thing: we press people to reconstruct the walls and crawl back inside them, often forcing the issue through excessive use of psychotropic drugs. Then we wonder why these folks continue to be miserable and to have recurrent breakdowns.

With the help of a loving extended family and the cautious use of medication, we were able to treat Mimi without hospitalizing her. I saw her several times each week at first, sometimes with her family. In addition to enlisting their help in the treatment, I wanted to prepare them for Vicki's inevitable and unpredictable changes. As the crisis passed we reduced the frequency of visits, decreased medication, and began couple therapy. The changes have been difficult for Tom, but he is learning to enjoy this funny, spirited and sensual woman, and to value the playfulness and amiability he is finding in himself in response to her. I still have on a shelf in my office the delightful wooden puppy that he carved for me.

The word *crazy* comes from the Old Norse word *kraza*, meaning to crack or break. It also has a very specific usage: when it is time for a bird to come out of its egg into life, it begins pecking from the inside. The pattern of cracks that forms all along the shell is called *kraza*.

To go crazy, to have a "breakdown," is to peck out of one's shell for the purpose of emerging into life.

The Art and the Science

Science without religion is lame. Religion without science is blind.
Albert Einstein

The division of intellectual life into art and science has become basic to literate society. It is said that our Western culture has two historical roots, one in Athens and the other in Jerusalem. So much of our civilization has been inherited, directly or indirectly, from the ancient Greeks and Israelites.

Athens has given us logic, analytic thinking, science, and the cult of the individual within the polis. From Jerusalem we inherit revelation, intuition, blessing, and the idea of community binding the individual. This is a vast simplification, but a useful one. Our culture is built on a blending of these two world-attitudes, and we instinctively sense an imbalance when one of them precludes the other.

In the past century these tendencies manifested in the ascendance of two diametrically different modes of thought: logical positivism and analytic philosophy on the one hand, and phenomenology and existentialism on the other. Immeasurable amounts of verbiage have been expended debating which of these is "more true". I think most of us would agree that neither can be neglected, any more than the right or left halves of our brains should be ignored.

We do, however, take both to extremes. In modern pop culture and in the medical field, Athens is often represented by an unreasoning faith in whatever is alleged to be "scientific", without much cognizance of the limits or the methodology of science. Jerusalem is reduced to a gullible search for meaning outside of science that often seems to accept any belief as true if it seems neat or trendy. In the name of wholeness, we need to get back to fundamentals. Neither passion nor critical thinking is expendable.

Psychology is a scientific study, while psychotherapy is a specialized form of the art of relationship. This is the difference between an objective investigation and a personal and kindhearted connection. Both are essential. To attempt psychotherapy without in-depth reference to psychological knowledge is to risk undisciplined vision, unexamined intuition, and the shattering of the other person in the force of our passion. Striving to be therapeutic through science alone leaves us in an arid wasteland of disconnected intellect.

As therapists, we must attend to the state of scientific knowledge in psychology. Our clients, however, are not very interested in that. They ask the living questions: Am I all right? How do I deal with my pain? What gives meaning to my life? How do I live in relationship? What does it mean to speak of spirit in my life, or of faith? As scientists will be happy to tell you, these questions are not addressed in scientific inquiry. Such inquiry bypasses entirely the fields of ethics, theology, esthetics, and anything else that is not about verifiable reality.

Science is the language of the material world, including psychology. Science is not the language of emotion or of experience, and thus it cannot be the language of psychotherapy. With hearts full of yearning, we turn to the language of art. Only the language of art can carry the full import of complexity, ambiguity, mystery, and above all abundance of meaning. These form the irreducible core of our experience: multidimensional rather than linear, metaphorical rather than literal, and abundant in significance and mystery.

When we need to convey life's experience, we turn to the language of art. I may offer a client interpretations regarding his fear of loss in a relationship, and his ambivalence about being close; this is an important piece of psychological understanding. When I then share with him—even silently—my own trembling at the doors of intimacy, my own sense of fear and fascination as I enter further into relationship, our dialogue is suddenly infused with life. Together, we experience our vulnerability and our longing.

Once we have done what we can through theory and technique, then the healing acts of psychotherapy must be conducted in the languages of poetry, metaphor, mime, storytelling, humor, movement, and other art forms—forms indefinitely defined, forms rich in the imprecision and multiplicity of experience, addressing the inner and shared life of this person standing in relation to us.

Science deals with things. It is an indispensable source of knowledge. In psychotherapy we encounter *persons*, and we learn to say *"Thou"*.

CHAPTER 10
PSYCHOTHERAPY AND NEUROSCIENCE

Ruth is telling me about her initial visit with a psychiatrist. Although she had not come seeking medication, he dismissed her after twenty minutes, prescription in hand. She protested, "I have a lot on my mind. Aren't you going to talk with me?" "No," he responded, "I don't do that."

This is a true story; I couldn't make it up.

Many members of the psychiatric profession have abandoned psychotherapy entirely, functioning as though psychiatry were about neurochemistry and nothing else. They see patients briefly, make medical-model diagnoses, and attend only to pharmaceutical symptom relief. The individual's personality and inner experience are barely acknowledged, and their patients feel anonymous and uncared for.

On the other side of the fence, too many psychotherapists are ill-trained to recognize biological factors that, untended, can bring therapy to a standstill. Their knowledge of elementary brain biology may be sketchy, resulting in a failure of holistic vision even among therapists who otherwise pride themselves on such thinking. This results in a lack of awareness, or even a blanket denial, of the importance of medical treatment for some clients.

The psychiatrists and the therapists are not speaking to one other, or even thinking in the same language. Everyone loses, and the client most of all. The language of neuroscience and the language of experience are indeed dissimilar; they need not be irreconcilable. Like those high-school math problems that could be expressed in words or in algebraic equations, they represent two different ways of apprehending one reality. Arguing over which one is "right" strikes me as trying to decide which of my two legs is the more important one.

Mind and Brain

To begin with the obvious: the species *Homo sapiens* is part of the animal kingdom.

We are unique animals, at least on this planet. We possess a huge quantity of brain, much of which is not needed to govern our bodies. This spare brain material makes us significantly smarter than everyone else around. Without it, we would be poorly suited for survival and reproductive success; we are slow, weak, and without natural weapons or armor. We don't reproduce quickly or easily, and our prolonged childhood would doom many other species to extinction. Perhaps most peculiarly, we are possessed of self-consciousness; we may be the only animal who is. My dog has no idea whom he sees in the mirror, and no thought of his own mortality.

For all the differences, we remain biological creatures; we neglect at our peril the mind's dependence on the brain. It is fascinating to watch as science explores, and increasingly understands, correlations between the biological events of the brain and the behavioral and subjective events of the mind and spirit. We know now that our brains continue evolving throughout life; learning and experience modify neuronal formation, synaptic connection and cellular communication, altering the anatomy itself.

Brain function is affected by nutrition, general health, hormone levels, inflammation and numerous other physical factors. Biology influences personality; personality and experience influence brain biology. If you take a drug or get sick, your disposition is affected. If you are depressed, contented, frightened or excited, it changes the way your brain operates, and over time the changes can become lasting. There is recent persuasive evidence, for example, that chronic depression leads to nerve cell atrophy and a communicative disorganization of neuronal networks.

Cognitive and biological studies demonstrate that the brain functions differently under stress, whether that stress consists of physical trauma, hormonal change, social and relational events, illness or disaster. Moderate levels of stress stimulate our brains, increasing comprehension, concentration, problem solving, creativity, memory-formation and other functions. Then at some point mounting stress becomes trauma, and functioning in every area decreases sharply. Sustained trauma becomes encoded in the microanatomy and neurochemistry of the brain, and that in turn influences future perception, behavior and decision-making.

Our lives are impelled not only by our inborn tendencies, but also by how we understand and manage those tendencies. Nature and nurture, mind and brain, chemistry and consciousness, are different perspectives from which to view a continuous and amazingly complex state of affairs.

Without attempting to become physicians, therapists do well to have at least a passing familiarity with the most common factors affecting metabolism, mood and cognitive functioning. These include (but are not limited to) diabetes, thyroid disease, allergy, the effects of corticosteroid and reproductive hormones, physical and emotional stress and trauma, alcohol and drugs, and some neurological disorders. In addition, it is important to acknowledge the biochemical and genetic factors in depression, anxiety, attention-deficit syndromes, schizophrenia and other entities that we encounter.

Finally, considerations about medication have become a daily and important part of our practices.

Better Living Through Chemistry?

I began in this profession with the opinion—or at least the prejudice—that all the healing could be done through the therapy relationship alone, and that medication was seldom necessary. Psychoanalytic training tended to reinforce that notion. Over time, my patients convinced me I was wrong.

In 1979, I had a small private practice outside of Boston. Alan, a very competent and compassionate pastoral counselor, asked me to consult with a young woman he had been seeing. During three years of therapy she had made considerable changes in her life, yet she remained as profoundly depressed as when they first met. He wondered what they were missing, and asked me to meet with her for re-evaluation.

Moira was bright, amiable and enjoyable to be with. At the end of our two-hour meeting, I had no idea what the problem was. Alan's assessment of her seemed accurate in every respect. It made no sense that she remained so deeply depressed.

I said, "Moira, I just don't know. You've been depressed and anxious at least since your teen years, and there's plenty in your background to account for that. But you've worked hard with a good therapist, you've improved every part of your life, and you seem to be living in a way that's true to yourself. You ought to feel better. I don't get it either.

"But I have a crazy intuition. I don't know how to understand it, but here it is.

"As you and I talk, I feel this odd, sinking sensation in my gut. It's the same feeling I get when I'm at the hospital talking with someone who is manic-depressive in the dark, depressed pit of suffering. I don't know what that means for you, since there's no evidence that you've ever been manic, just this awful depression. But the feeling in my belly is strong.

"We treat those people with Lithium, and it often gives them enormous relief. I honestly don't know what I'm doing here, but I'd like to play a hunch. I wonder if you'd be willing to try the same treatment."

Moira agreed—said, in fact, she'd try anything. We discussed the medication and I wrote her a prescription.

When I saw her two weeks later, she was a changed person. I was amazed at her appearance; she was astounded at how she felt. In a bright mood for the first time in 15 years, she reported an unaccustomed clarity of thought and a sense of peace. The mild side effects she experienced in the first few days had faded away. I heard now an astonishing statement that I've listened to many times since: "This feels like the way I was supposed to be."

My experience with Moira and with others has driven me—without diminishing the value of therapy—to advocate a crucial place for psychotropic medication. Moira had a genetically predisposed biological condition, an alteration of brain chemistry. She was simply not going to find relief without addressing this condition medically. No amount of therapy and life-change could entirely alleviate her mood disorder.

A surprising number of our clients suffer from neurochemical disorders that produce psychological symptoms. The therapeutic ideal in these situations is a combination of psychotherapy and medical treatment. Treating these folks with therapy alone, or with medication alone, leaves a crucial part of the problem unaddressed.

The human brain is an amazing thing. The world's most complex computer, it is manufactured entirely by unskilled labor. Roughly the size of half a grapefruit, it contains somewhere between 50 and 100 billion neurons. The average neuron makes about 10,000 synaptic connections, mostly to other neurons, some to muscles and various organs. At these junctions, messages are relayed over microscopic distances by chemicals called neurotransmitters, including glutamate, serotonin, norepinephrin, and dopamine (there are many more). In addition, neurons and synapses are subject to multiple influences from within and without the brain. The number of possible combinations, biochemical states, and configurations of neural networks is virtually unlimited. Add in the countless possibilities provided by heredity and random variation, and every person is truly a singular and irreplaceable individual.

Incidentally, only one to two percent of these 100 billion neurons are involved in rational thinking. All the rest are doing other things. Like it or not, we are not fundamentally rational creatures.

In psychotherapy, we hope to provide new experiences that will modify the effects of previous experience. The brain encodes these new experiences by reconfiguring synaptic interaction and neuronal networks, thus influencing future emotion, cognition and behavior.

Psychotherapy is a powerful tool for changing the brain as well as the disposition. After a successful course of therapy, we may experience ourselves in some important ways as different people. In neurobiological terms, that is literally true.

But it is not always enough. For people like Moira, the genetic determinants, potentiated by the experience of being chronically depressed (or anxious, paranoid, or whatever), cannot be entirely overcome by new experience. Then the disordered neurochemistry must be addressed directly.

Most clients come to us for reasons that are not primarily rooted in biological or genetic causes. They generally do well in psychotherapy, and for the most part it would be unnecessary and unwise to introduce medication into the equation. On the other hand, some of them suffer severe physiological symptoms like anorexia, insomnia, debilitating fatigue, panic attacks, headaches and other painful ailments. Some will be struggling with self-destructive impulses. In such cases, simple humanity demands that relief with medication be a serious consideration.

One oft-heard objection is the assertion that drugs are a way of avoiding responsibility for one's life. Certainly that can be the case. But when medication is used appropriately, just the opposite is true. You *are* responsible for your life. Symptoms can leave you out of control, and an important goal of medication is to put you back in charge, to give you more flexibility and more choices. As one very articulate individual expressed it to me, "It was like I was going through life with chains on my ankles. The medication took the chains off. I've still had to do all the walking."

The Therapist as Advocate

Unfortunately, many physicians—even psychiatrists—spend little time talking with, or listening to, their patients. Follow-up on psychotropic medication may be sketchy or non-existent. These regrettable tendencies have been further aggravated by the current economics of health care (don't even get me started!). For our purposes, this means that your client on medication often must rely on you for a certain amount of monitoring.

Ask the questions: How does this medication affect you? Do you feel different? Better, worse, or about the same? What is the medicine doing for you? What isn't it doing? Any side effects, such as sedation, nausea, irritability, etc.? Is there a downside to taking it? Have you seen your doctor? Is it affecting your sexual response? Do you feel like yourself? Can you think clearly? How is your energy? If there is change, are you experiencing a normal range of emotions, or is it making you numb?

Many people just assume that they must accept some side effects (especially emotional or sexual blunting, which is *not* an acceptable result). Clients should be encouraged to let their doctors know; most side-effects can be reduced or eliminated by judicious management of the medication. If their doctor isn't interested, encourage them to be more assertive, or to consider getting another opinion.

As mood and cognition improve, people may be confused about their experience. Your client may inquire, "I think I'm feeling calmer since I started this medicine, but I'm still very sad. Does that mean it isn't working?" In response, we need to help her look at her life, to separate the situational from the biological.

Natalie has been coming to therapy for about a year, and it has gone well. She has also had a nice response to medication for her chronic depression and anxiety. But last evening she drank way too much wine and found herself lying on her living room floor and crying uncontrollably for two hours. Her first thought was that her medication was no longer working.

I asked if she could think of any circumstance in her life to account for this; at first she couldn't. I wondered about her mother's death just two months earlier. She didn't think that was it, for their relationship had been distant and she hadn't felt much grief.

Still, I knew about her family life. The oldest of six sibs, she had been the stand-in for an absent father and an ineffectual, alcoholic mother. Now she was once again the responsible one; she made the funeral arrangements, worked with the attorneys, closed Mother's house, and tended to her brothers and her sister.

As often happens, the responsible one had been the last to have time or liberty to grieve.

As we spoke of this, Natalie became tearful and very sad. She began to experience her grief: the forlorn hope of someday having a good relationship had died with her mother. The wine and her fatigue had lowered her defenses, and she had begun, belatedly, to mourn.

The client needs to see whether her situation warrants sadness, and if it seems proportional. Further, can she tell the difference between sadness and depression? People often do not understand that depression is a symptom, but some sadness is part of life.

It may be important to explain that *the opposite of depression is not happiness. The opposite of depression is vitality, the energy and capacity to get on with life.* And life inevitably includes some loss, sadness, anxiety, grief, frustration and anger. Some of that can be mitigated, while some simply needs to be endured.

Above all, the client should feel that his medication is enabling him to get on with life. He should sense that it allows him to be himself; *the change should be restorative, not forced or cosmetic.* Otherwise, it should be re-assessed. Again, encourage him to discuss this with the prescribing physician. He may be intimidated about asking questions or "bothering" his doctor. Without your support he may accept an unsatisfactory result, or just stop taking medication that he needs.

Discussion of these issues in therapy often leads us into other important matters. The way in which a person relates to medication is often characteristic of his relationships with significant people in his life. He may approach medication thoughtfully or impulsively, cautiously or recklessly; he may be curious and self-responsible, dependent, afraid or passively resisting. He may show ongoing ambivalence, timidity, suspicion, appreciation, resentment or collaboration. Watch for the same qualities in his relationships with you and others.

•

Who, then, prescribes for your client?

When I began my first rotation on obstetrics as a junior medical student, one of the attendings explained to our little group just what we were doing there. "The corner cop can deliver the baby," she said, "That is, as long as it's a routine, uncomplicated delivery. But they are not all routine and uncomplicated. That's what you people are here for."

Any physician is legally entitled to write a prescription for any medication. On the other hand, as a psychiatrist I never prescribe antibiotics; one can't do that properly without spending a great deal of energy staying current.

If you come to my office complaining of recurrent chest pain, I will not do a cardiogram or institute treatment for heart disease. It's not because I don't know about those things; when I did general medicine, it was routine. But that's not what I do now, and I'm rusty and out of touch. I no longer know the fine points. I will refer you to an internist or a cardiologist.

A wise physician sticks to what he or she knows. Non-psychiatric physicians are not equipped to make accurate diagnoses in this field. Nor do they have the time it requires; I do this every day, and I will not prescribe until I have spent an hour or more with someone. These physicians, often highly competent in their own areas, are unfamiliar with psychopathology and with the particulars of these types of medication, and they do not know how and when to follow up.

Some therapists will do the evaluation and then send the patient to his family doctor for the prescription, even suggesting which medication to prescribe. You may do a good evaluation and make an accurate psychological diagnosis, but are you prepared to manage the medication, its place in the client's overall health profile, and any complications that arise? That's what you'd be doing, since his usual physician hasn't the experience.

Along with competence and experience, what do you want from your medical consultant?

First, bear in mind that the use of medication takes place in a relationship, or a set of relationships. It begins with the doctor-patient alliance, and extends to the patient's therapist, family members, friends and workplace. Ideally, the physician will bear in mind the client's social and family circumstances, intervening religious or cultural considerations, the relationship with the therapist, and the patient's previous experience with other practitioners.

You want someone who will spend the necessary time with your client, make a careful and thoughtful diagnosis, and hopefully gain his confidence. You want to know that the client will be seen and reassessed at appropriate times, and that the physician will be available as needed. You want a consultant who will not medicate too quickly or too randomly, and who may sometimes say, "I don't think medication is in order. Your work with your therapist will give you the tools you need." Not everyone should be taking medications, and many people are grateful when told they don't need them.

At best, we hope for a three-way relationship of client, therapist and physician that is characterized by collaboration, accurate and plentiful information, and respect for the needs of each of the actors. Ideals are not always reality. You may have to settle for less, in some cases a lot less. But the closer you can get, the better.

The Politics of Medication

This is a troublesome subject that we can't avoid. Our thinking about medication must account for the real-world context in which we operate: the American pharmaceutical industry, along with the political and economic structures that currently support it. So hold your nose; we're about to visit the smelly eight-hundred-pound gorilla.

Drugs are expensive and becoming more so all the time. Some of this cost genuinely reflects the high-tech nature of today's medicines, but other (sometimes embarrassing) factors are hidden behind convenient myths.

Myth number one: drug prices reflect real market influences. The fact is that drug companies receive many special non-competitive breaks from our lawmakers, and anti-trust laws are winked at all the time. The major pharmaceutical companies have the largest profit margin of any industry in this country, estimated at 18-25% per annum (compare with the average for other Fortune-500 companies, at 3.3%). In its business dealings, the industry is almost unregulated.

The most glaring example or special favors is the 2003 Medicare drug prescription program. This law bars Medicare from the normal business practice of using its huge numbers of insured people to negotiate for lower prices. According to the non-partisan Congressional Budget Office, the average Medicare price for the fifty medications most prescribed for senior citizens comes to $1500 per patient per year. The Veterans Administration, which *does* observe this elementary business principle, pays an average of $322 (one fifth as much!) for the same drugs; this is comparable to the prices in Europe, Japan and Canada.

The pharmaceutical companies are in business to make money. This is not a bad thing; the free-market system has improved our lives beyond reckoning. The problem is that health care does not conform to the same market model as the sale of television sets, kitchen knives or athletic shoes. It is *not* a market governed primarily by voluntary and rational selection; decisions are often made in fear, desperation, pain and ignorance. Demand is intermittent and unpredictable, and "market choice" is for the most part a fantasy. Additionally, the consumer doesn't know what he needs, and must rely on the physician to tell him.

Myth number two: safety concerns dictate that we not import drugs from other countries, such as Canada. Fact: many of the drugs we would be importing (or re-importing) were manufactured right here. It is also the case that the standards of the Canadian government (and several others, including Great Britain, Switzerland, France and Germany) are comparable to ours.

Curiously, safety did not seem to be an issue when our government contracted with British firms for the manufacture of influenza vaccine. And when the supply fell short during the flu season of 2004-2005, there was no hesitation in bringing in vaccine from other countries, including France.

Myth number three: drug prices remain high in order to fund research. It is true that the research behind a new drug can be pricey. But we must ask how often new research is involved, and who actually foots the bill?

According to medical market expert Marcia Angell, MD, (Harvard faculty and former Chief Editor of the New England Journal of Medicine), in 2002 the top ten pharmaceutical companies totaled sales of 217 billion dollars. Of this sum, $150 billion went to marketing and distribution (think direct-consumer TV advertising, and also the extensive four-color advertising thrown daily at your doctor). That leaves *$37 billion in profit*, as well as an average CEO salary in excess of $10 million per year. $30 billion, or just 14%, was spent on research, a good deal less than the profit margin, and very little of this was the basic research that results in new treatments.

Well, then, where do all the new drugs come from?

To begin with, only 15% of "new" drugs are actually new, i.e. based on newly discovered active ingredients. The rest consists mainly of new packaging, newly marketed dosages, or new indications for existing drugs (usually discovered by doctors in clinical practice). Then there are the "me too" drugs, by which a company tries to gain its own market share with a drug that does the same thing as drugs that are already available.

It should also be noted that (again according to Dr. Angell) approximately 15% of all basic pharmaceutical research is actually financed by major pharmaceutical companies. Most of the remaining 85% is supported by government or university money—your tax dollars at work. A smaller portion is done by small, private biotech firms.

This is a quick glimpse of the American pharmaceutical industry. It's capitalism run amok, and it's costing us all. It's not a pretty sight.

Ethical Considerations

This is a complex subject, with tendrils in all of medical and psychotherapeutic ethics. I will confine myself to a few observations here. More on ethics in our final chapter.

When I began a career in psychiatry in 1969, the medications available to us were relatively crude. Most were "shotgun" treatments, affecting numerous neurochemical pathways and generating a variety of non-specific effects on brain and other organs. Many were marginally efficacious, and most were accompanied by an abundant supply of side effects. This made it easy to favor drug-free psychotherapy for all but the most psychotic patients.

Since then the astonishing advances in neuropharmacology, along with the increasing understanding of the role of brain biology in affect, cognition and temperament, have abolished that luxury. Some of today's drugs are dramatic in their potential for enhancing one's balance and well being. Many (the serotonergic agents, in particular) work not by masking symptoms, but by restoring healthy neural functioning.

The use of drugs in any medical specialty is never a simple judgment. Every decision is a balancing act between the potential good and the potential harm to be done.

As physicians will tell you, the most important principle in the practice of medicine is "Do no harm." That principle implies rejecting remedies that are likely to do more ill than good (hold the leaches!), and there are many patients who are better off without medication. But that principle also commands us not to neglect beneficial treatment. Advising somebody against the use of needed psychotropic medication can be as reckless as refusing insulin to a diabetic.

As psychotherapists, our task is not to dictate who someone should be, but to liberate him to be who he is. This notion also provides a guidepost with regard to psychotropics. If a drug interferes with the living of a full life, perhaps through sedation or emotional or sexual dulling, that medication must be reassessed. But if it is helping the individual to get on with his therapy and his life, it is misguided to dissuade him.

The fact of medication calls upon us to wrestle with the conundrum of "chemical sanity". I think of Cheryl and her refusal "to take drugs" in the face of her growing psychosis. She, like others, rejected medication for fear that she would lose her self. Does relief and clarity through medication mean that one is no longer oneself? If one needs medication to be sane, doesn't this call into question the very idea of sanity? Yet despite these agonizing doubts, I cannot disregard the experience of watching her gradually deteriorate, slowly fading, leaving behind a being who is inaccessible, unfathomable and seemingly less than whole as a human being. What dreadful thing has happened when Cheryl is no longer here?

Sometimes I am compelled to return to the subject of medication even in the face of the individual's misgivings. I must step as best I can around her fear and resistance, trying to minimize suspicion and anger. I must overcome my own reflexive reluctance to medicate, for I cannot in good conscience allow myself to ignore the subject even when my patient asks me to. The consequences of neglecting what is in front of me can be catastrophic. I can see that Lisa is losing patience with me, so I put the topic aside for a time. But it is clear that she will not be able to live the life she wants, free of her relentless terror and profound melancholia, without including medication in her therapy. I have no responsible choice but to return to the subject, even at the risk of having her leave treatment.

How do we answer questions of life and meaning while still maintaining an empirical and scientific perspective? And how do we keep our sense of rationality without strangling our souls? If we romanticize the client's struggle, seeing it solely as high tragedy or a journey of transformation, we allow ourselves to be pried loose from the reality of his suffering. But if we see his yearnings only as illness, we ignore the animation of his spirit, and of our own with it.

CHAPTER 11
THE INTIMATE BONDS: COUPLES AND FAMILIES

The two most difficult and complex careers that most of us tackle are being in a marriage and raising children. No one teaches us much about how these things are done. We are always starting from scratch, and there is no shame in seeking help with either vocation.

In an important sense, all therapy is family therapy. We bring with us all the significant people in our lives, past and present. The room is crowded with them; they teem and swarm, noisily demanding our attention. They pop up when expected and when least expected. The crowd fills the office, at times consuming all the air. They can hardly be ignored. It has been truly said that family therapy is not just about the people in the room, but about the people in the minds of therapist and client.

Conceptual models for understanding family relationships—systems theory, for example—have made invaluable contributions to our work. They add entire dimensions to the classical intrapsychic focus, enabling the other eye of our binocular vision. But intellectual caution is in order; overemphasis on "systems", without reference to the subjective experience of individuals, can become excessively behavioral, ignoring personal meaning and the emotional and spiritual dimensions of events.

From a systems perspective, family events can be seen as collusion: "the family" decides that Mother can't tolerate certain kinds of information, so everyone (including Mother) conspires to keep her ignorant and protected. This implies a kind of systemic consciousness, as if the system itself were a creature with a goal or purpose. While this is descriptively vivid, attributing intent to the group is like characterizing biological evolution as having a goal; in fact it is a series of individual events interacting as a system that can behave "as if" there were a conscious purpose.

We can watch family members respond to relational events each in his or her own way, and these responses become complimentary and reinforcing. The individuals interact in discernible cycles, each of them doing what they do because it's what they know to do. "The system" does not have a goal or purpose. It only behaves *as if* it did.

PART I: THERAPY WITH COUPLES

What is Marriage?

Anthropologists tell us that some form of marriage is nearly universal, originating first and foremost in the need to care for a population of helpless human infants and children.

The belief that marriage has always been "between one man and one woman" simply doesn't fit the facts. Approximately 80% of the societies studied by anthropologists allow polygyny: one man may have several wives. This group includes a number of modern societies in the Islamic, East Asian, and African world. It is true that multiple marriage is practiced by only a small minority in each culture, for the simple reason that most men can't afford it. (There are only five known societies that allow polyandry.)

Those who claim that one man, one woman marriage is the only Biblically accepted form have apparently skipped parts of the Bible. Many of the men, including the patriarchs Abraham and Jacob, and most of the Israelite kings, had more than one wife. (Solomon is said to have had hundreds. This is wise?)

In most societies marriage is not between a man and a woman, but between their two families, or between the man and the woman's father. Marriage for love is a recent development, and in much of the world today it is still thought to be a bad idea, an invitation to family instability. Even in current American society we don't *really* insist on "one man, one woman"; there is widespread acceptance of divorce and serial monogamy. While we still disapprove of adultery, there is in practice some tolerance of it, and most people no longer consider it sufficient reason to end a marriage.

It is true that same-sex marriage is virtually unheard of until recently. This has not always been a moral issue, for many societies have been more accepting of homosexual relationships than ours. It appears that same-sex marriage hasn't been an issue simply because it has had no value for the survival of children; it arises now in a time of changing circumstances and social ideas.

When we discuss marriage today, we find ourselves amid a babble of conflicting voices and opinions. Much of the confusion occurs because we are talking about several different visions of marriage as if they were one, or as if there could be only one.

When the words "love, honor and obey" became part of the vows, they served as a pithy expression of the ancient and traditional view of marriage. Love referred primarily to conventional religious, family and community obligations, and had little to do with romance, eros or intimacy. The courtly ideal of passionate and redeeming love arose only in the late middle ages, and was incompatible with marriage as traditionalists saw it; romance occurred outside of marriage, and was often adulterous. Think Lancelot and Guinevere, or Tristram and Iseult, or *The Bridges of Madison County*.

Today we have some different ideas about marriage. We have redefined it as a deeply personal and profoundly intimate relationship that includes passion, friendship and the erotic. In this wished-for state, commitment is created not only by religious and social vows, but also by the living love in the relationship.

We expect marriage to be an ongoing sacrament of generosity, forgiveness, sexuality and regeneration. We long for a covenant of renewed purpose, respect and affirmation. One's partner is seen not as a set of functions and expectations, but as a fully valid human being.

What a colossal set of expectations! No wonder so many of today's marriages crumble. We ask so much of them, and we are ill prepared for the tasks they require.

Yet this ideal is not an impossible one. Some couples do learn to live this way. It requires maturity, realism, perseverance, judgment and wisdom. Most of us reach adult life poorly equipped for this. Hopefully we learn.

Same-Sex Marriage?

We can't entirely separate our therapeutic endeavors from questions of public policy. Nowhere is this more the case than in a discussion of marriage. One of the basic hopes of therapy is the promotion of family stability, and this is also a fundamental purpose of marriage.

If we are interested in strengthening families, then we must do those things that actually empower and protect families, encouraging responsibility and commitment. At this time we have a group of people (previously condemned for their alleged instability and promiscuity) who are asking to marry; they wish to formalize and shelter their commitments to each other and their families, which often include their children. If we truly wish to promote the values of loyalty, fidelity and family, why are we denying these folk the right to legitimize and protect their unions? Our current models of marriage, with our hopes of personal, emotional and sexual fulfillment, give us every reason to include these couples.

The contention that allowing two men or two women to legitimate their relationship "will jeopardize traditional marriage" is a slogan, not a reasoned social position. I have not noticed that heterosexual marriage has been an unqualified success, nor can I see that my marriage is in any danger from the union of those two nice girls down the street. We can live agreeably side-by-side. These folks are not *threatening* a traditional institution; they are asking to *join* it.

Justifications of heterosexual-only marriage on the basis of procreation alone makes sense only if we believe that the bearing of children is the single valid justification for marriage; that companionship, intimacy, support and the joining of two spirits before man and God are not sufficient reason. If this is your position, think carefully: it implies that we should give our political leaders absolute power to regulate family planning, pre-marital sex, and gynecologic surgery. It would also forbid the marriage of all infertile people, including post-menopausal women and men with vasectomies.

I genuinely sympathize with those of you whose religious convictions do not allow you to consider same-sex unions as matrimony. While our religious convictions may inform us as people and as citizens, our therapeutic vocation demands that we treat these couples like any others. Whatever your opinion on the legal issues, we owe them the honor due to every couple who seeks us out. If you are personally averse to acknowledging a same-sex couple as a *de facto* marriage, you must excuse yourself from seeing these people; to do otherwise would be untrue both to you and to the couple. But please refer them, and gently. They do not deserve judgment or censure over who they are.

A Framework: Five Relational Tasks for Couples

If a union is to be successful, there are crucial relational tasks to be learned and practiced. When people come to us hoping for a more loving and rewarding relationship, mindfulness of these tasks can provide an overall vision for the work. Not surprisingly, these relational tasks are also those required in the "marriage" of therapist and client.

First task: Learning to be a grownup

We will meet disappointment in our lives. At best we will get some of what we want. Learning to be a grownup means taking life on its own terms, with its limitations and losses. It means accepting imperfection and disappointment. It means rising above our frustrations with generosity and love. This is not easy, and it takes much practice.

Ray has been talking about his persistent anger toward his wife. When they were engaged he reluctantly promised he would be faithful to her. He did not express his misgivings, fearing—most likely correctly—that she would not marry him. Now he is continually enraged with her for preventing the dalliances he desires. Twice he has strayed secretly. Either Ray will learn to stop blaming her and be responsible for his own decisions, or he will destroy his marriage in a most painful way.

Being accountable for oneself is the most important part of being a grownup. We must learn to be answerable for ourselves rather than blaming things, circumstances, or our partners for our unhappiness or our behavior ("I wouldn't have done that if she hadn't..."). We must acknowledge our mistakes and lapses, and look for our own part in any problem. When confession and apology are necessary we do so with contrition and a desire to learn, not just to escape consequences. Criticism, defensiveness and resentment are behaviors that corrode and destroy relationships.

Second task: Acceptance

Acceptance begins with the decision not to judge. This is the very heart of loving behavior. I embrace this person as she is, with her contradictions, quirks and imperfections. I resolve that love and respect are her birthright, and I do not place conditions on it. I accept who she is even when her decisions and behaviors are inconvenient for me.

Acceptance means deciding to overcome my self-absorption, my narcissism. I acknowledge that she was not put in the world to take care of me, and I may not expect her to sacrifice her integrity to meet my needs. My desires are not laws of nature. To say this another way, I choose relationship over ego.

Loving acceptance must be *unconditional*. To be unconditional is to say that love is *unearned*. There is nothing she has to do to deserve it.

This does not mean that I discount or demean myself, nor will I accept being treated badly. Cruelty, disrespect, intentional injury and betrayal are not tolerable. Unconditional acceptance of the other is not disregard for myself. If something is hurtful to me, I owe it to her and to myself to speak up, to give voice to my experience or my request for change, and to do so while avoiding criticism. *Acceptance means protesting within the relationship rather than from the ego, without self-righteousness, contempt or retaliation.*

The relational way entails addressing our differences with respect and seeking a caring resolution. *Acceptance is a choice; anger an indication that something needs attention.* Unconditional acceptance creates a relationship that can endure through times of misunderstanding, frustration and discomfort.

Third task: Practicing generosity

Conjugal love cannot be based solely on need. Need is rooted in scarcity, threat, loss or emptiness. You need comfort, shelter, affection and food. When someone provides these things for you, you may be grateful. You may have warm feelings for him or want to return the favor. This is not the same as loving. "I need you" is not "I love you."

Love is about giving, not needing. If you are consumed with need or fear, you are in the relationship because you must be. When you act from generosity, you give what the other needs. Then you can be with him because you *want* to be, not because you must.

Practicing generosity can be difficult, especially when we have experienced deprivation. When we feel empty, we expect that giving will leave us more depleted. Generosity demands an act of faith and will. It often enjoins the desire to overcome our own past and to do better for those we love. When we do that, giving becomes a vibrant reality. Rather than filling emptiness, you are there to share fullness.

Fourth task: Forgiveness

There will be wounds in personal relationships. We hurt each other carelessly, or deliberately, or defensively. Healing those wounds requires asking for and offering forgiveness. I can be certain that in any lengthy relationship I will have many opportunities both to ask and to give pardon.

Forgiveness in marriage comes in two forms. The first is forgiveness for actual transgressions, as small as an irritable flare-up or as large as a breach of trust. There must be genuine regret and a sincere desire to correct the offense.

Then (but only then) the partner must somehow find forgiveness. An injury unrepented is a continuing wound.

Forgiveness does not mean forgetting. To forgive is not to say that what happened is all right, or that it can be put out of mind. To forgive is to let go, to accept that what has happened is done and need not control our lives now. *Forgiveness consists of the willingness to put the injury in the past and allow healing to occur.*

The second form of marital forgiveness is the acknowledgment of our partners as human and limited. We must forgive each other for being unable to meet all needs or to make life blissful. It is not enough merely to allow the partner's shortcomings; we must do so without bitterness, resentment or martyrdom. When we love someone, we embrace them without playing victim, being sacrificial or keeping score.

Fifth task: Risking intimacy

Intimacy is elemental to our hopes for marriage. Some couples come to therapy precisely because of a lack of intimacy. Others come for different reasons, but turn in this direction once the initial crisis is surmounted. So just what do we mean when we speak of intimacy?

What we do *not* mean is romance. Romance is a breathless state, a rapture that descends on us from the heavens. It is magical: we *find the right one* and we *fall in love*. Bliss follows.

Anyone who has experienced the wild power of a deep infatuation knows its capacity to lift us outside ourselves. It is an ecstatic blend of projections, dreams, hopes, longings, hormones and fantasies. It feels like salvation. Everything we desire seems to lie before us for the taking, and we reject or ignore any evidence to the contrary. Just try telling someone in love that this person is not right for her. Romantic love truly is blind, because it is not grounded in who this person *is*.

To our sorrow, romance cannot last. With time and experience, the beloved emerges as a real person, and the fantasy begins to unravel. This is not salvation after all. There is no happily ever after.

Now the work begins. Romance has not prepared us for the effort and the risk of intimacy. Our dreams of perfection persuaded us that there was no need for such struggle; love conquers all. Now we enter a relationship of two real people, with its need for acceptance, forgiveness and generosity. Now we leave romance and begin to become intimate.

When we are intimate, we are engaged in the anxious but joyful act of being individually whole while being genuinely present with the other person. This requires openness, acceptance, and the willingness to be vulnerable. There must be recognition of separation and difference, and there must be authenticity and integrity on the part of both partners.

Fusion, also spoken of as enmeshment, is sometimes mistaken for intimacy; there is an important difference. In a fused relationship each partner perceives the other as being crucial to his or her survival. If you are necessary for my continued existence, I will do whatever is needed to keep you with me. I will stifle self-expression if that's what it takes. I will live a counterfeit existence, trying to be the person I think you want me to be. This is not intimacy, but dependence. Intimacy requires the acceptance of the entire, unique and separate human being.

This openness raises a particular difficulty: when people are distinct and individual, there will be conflict. Many of us are taught that conflict is inescapably dangerous. Yet acknowledging difference and disagreement is crucial for intimacy. When therapists teach couples to stifle conflict—for example with artificial compromises—we help them avoid intimacy. We do better to teach them to deal with differences openly and cleanly, with respect for their own and each other's truths.

In intimacy each partner stands in his/her abundant humanity, loving, revealing and appreciating, but singular. There are spaces in their closeness, latitude for individual as well as shared living. Without the recognition and celebration of difference there may be closeness but not intimacy, mutuality but not autonomy, comfort but not joy.

The intimate statement is not that I feel good when I am with you; there may be many reasons for that. More importantly, it is not that I like the person I am when I am with you; that implies that who I am depends on you. The genuinely intimate statement is this: When I am with you it is safe to be the person I truly am. I can share with you the joy of my being and of yours.

Binocular Family Vision

Along with the dynamics of the interplay, we want to account for each partner's personal experience. We can't afford the oversimplification of saying, "It is the couple that is my client." That's true, but it is also true that each individual is my client.

While the therapist observes and comments on the behavioral interactions and the mutually reinforcing cycles, he must also be present with each partner as an individual, as each encounters events in his or her own idiosyncratic ways, influenced by biology, social context, past experience, and human randomness and variation.

No one enters marriage with a blank slate; we bring our history, our other relationships, the influences of our original families and of everyone else that has shaped us, and all the real and misperceived experiences with the partner. We react not only to events, but also to the meanings we attach to those events. Having the individual *and* the partner see how the past shapes or distorts the present can be a powerful catalyst for changing perceptions.

Much is to be gained by asking each to accept the other's experience as real and significant. I may not always understand, and certainly I won't always agree, with my partner's perceptions and experiences. Sometimes we are just too different for that. What is essential is the acceptance of that subjectivity as valid and meaningful.

When you raise your voice, I think you are attacking me; that's what I learned in my family. When I understand that you come from a huge and noisy household where speaking below a shout meant not being heard at all, my defensiveness may diminish as I understand that it isn't all about me. Or if I still feel threatened, I can learn that I don't have to counterattack; I can simply say that I'm feeling anxious or defensive.

Sharing such information allows each to bear witness for the other. Bearing witness increases safety, teaches new ways to communicate, and makes more room for intimacy.

While identifying in therapy the interactions and the mutually reinforcing cycles, we will shift our attention from one partner to the other. We point out behaviors that perpetuate their frustration and misunderstanding, asking each in turn to look within or to try something different. We try to be clear, both with ourselves and the couple, that we are not taking sides, nor are we labeling either partner as being "the problem". It is, rather, an attempt to clear the obstacles that keep people stuck. Each individual has ways of perceiving, reacting and behaving, and any of these may be impediments or aids to change. Bringing these roadblocks to consciousness can point the way to new choices.

The Therapist with Couples

Even more obviously than most, couple therapy is relationship therapy. As soon as the couple is engaged in the work, the therapist becomes part of their union. Who we are, and the attitudes we manifest, become crucial elements for stasis or change.

This raises again the issue of congruence: each of us must do couple therapy in ways that fit our personalities and our life experiences. If your strongest suit is cognitive, then your best work may come as a kind of teaching; if you rely more on intuition and empathy, your approach will be different. You may be most effective seeing just the couple, or you may be doing your best when you bring in other family, or when you alternate the two.

I am often asked whether and when it is helpful to see members of a couple separately. I can only answer: it depends. I do not know the couple you're working with, and—even more importantly—I am not you. There is no universal answer, no formulaic procedure, for every therapist in every situation. Those who advocate prescriptive psychotherapy lead us down the path of impersonal standardization and superficiality. Instead, listen to what others have to say, and to the fruits of their experience. Attend to your couple, to their needs, fears, hopes and pains. Pay attention to your own associations, emotions and intuitions. Try different things and take suggestions from those you respect. *Then do what works for you.*

Certain questions can clarify early on just what the three of you are doing there: What sort of marriage do you want? What's missing that you would like? If we got a good result, how do you imagine it might look?

What would you hope from your partner? What are you willing to give? Is your current behavior getting you what you want? Are you willing to work on your own changes, or are you just expecting your partner to become different?

As the therapist, remind yourself that *the continuation of the marriage cannot be your responsibility.* I sometimes explain that I don't do marriage counseling; I do therapy with couples. For many people the phrase "marriage counseling" evokes the image of an all-knowing adviser who instructs the couple what to do, always with the goal of fixing the marriage. I decline that mission; it seems presumptuous to me. I will do my best to help them see the changes they could make; whether they choose to do so will be their decision. I freely admit that I have my bias: I think marriage can be a very good thing, and I am happy to see couples work through difficulties and end up contented with themselves and their relationship. I will try not to let my preferences get in the way of their therapy and the choices they make about their lives.

Differences

The single most important fact about couples is that we choose partners who are different from us. Most commonly this divergence is at the heart of a couple's difficulties, and constitutes the most crucial element of their therapy.

We like the romantic notion that we are drawn to each other because of all that we have in common. During the initial drama of attraction, lust and excitement, there is some truth to this: it is part of the "soulmate" fantasy.

The deeper truth is that the shared qualities are often peripheral to our personalities, like a fondness for exercise, theater or Japanese food. In the shadowy and less conscious realms of the mind, we choose people who complement us; they are rich in qualities that we are lacking.

The complimentarity shows up in many ways. The man who is of an analytic mind but short on emotive expressiveness is likely to choose a partner who relies on feeling and intuition. He is a problem solver while she is more sensitive to process and relationship. She needs his practicality and dependability; he benefits from her insight and passion.

The woman who is skilled at guiding and disciplining children may find herself with a husband with a talent for nurturing and playfulness. She chastises him for being too lax; he complains about her austerity.

After a while together we recognize—and are surprised by—how different we are. What do we do at that point? Well, we criticize our partners. We try to change them. We fight over who is right and who is the better person. He resents what he sees as her illogical emotional reactions, while she fusses about how he "just doesn't get it." We insist on making ourselves miserable because our partners are unlike us. We do battle over our differences instead of learning to share and enjoy them. We let them generate hostility and contempt instead of laughter.

Accepting our differences is the first key to a flourishing relationship. We can learn to treat those differences with creativity and humor. We are inherently funny creatures, and we generate endless opportunities for wry wit and irony.

Dealing with difference is often about managing frustration and learning to be a grownup. Grownups can live with disappointment without taking refuge in anger and blame. It is about holding onto a personal and loving perspective instead of falling into the childlike patterns that come so easily to all of us. We can take joy in our differences and learn from each other. The contrasts can provide background for playfulness, honesty, amusement and personal integrity. *While it is important to ask for changes in behavior, we must not ask our partners to change who they are.*

We must assume our partners are different until shown otherwise. We vary as much in perception and motivation as we do in size, shape and color. I will be sitting with a couple and one of them knows for certain the other's thoughts and motives. "He thinks I'm treating him like his mother!" Hearing this, he looks startled; that was nowhere in his mind. "She didn't register the checks in the book 'cause she wanted to piss me off." Turns out she didn't record the checks because he had moved the book and she couldn't find it.

Lee and Sandy are going out. As he emerges from the bedroom, she asks, "Are you wearing jeans to the movie?" Lee doesn't answer, but goes back to the bedroom. He reappears dressed in slacks, and Sandy is puzzled. She has no idea why he changed. He thought she was saying, "You're not going in jeans, are you?" But she just wanted to know; if he was going in jeans, so would she.

When we are sure we know what our partners think or feel, we are very likely to be wrong. Things hold different meanings for each of us. You are seeing events through your eyes, your unique set of feelings, your understandings and experiences. Mine are different. I cannot expect you to know what something means to me or how I feel about it unless I find a way to tell you.

The corollary to this is that we must ask for what we want. Ellen and Max have been living together only a few months. She gets home from work an hour before he does. When he arrives he putters around for a while, reads his mail and watches the six o'clock news. Ellen complains about this in our session; she feels insulted. She says that if he really cared for her he would come find her and give her a kiss. Max is surprised; his parents didn't do that and it never occurred to him. "I can do that," he says. "I didn't know you wanted me to." And he does.

So often we hear:
"He should know that I..."
"If she cared, she would..."
"I know the reason he didn't send a birthday card was..."
"When she makes that face, she's thinking..."

Most dangerous of all: "I shouldn't have to ask." And its close cousin, "If I have to ask, it isn't worth it!"

We are different. I can't say that enough. We do not just *know*. We must be taught. If I want my partner to know me, I must be willing to tell her about me. If I want to understand her, I must get curious and be prepared to listen. *Love is caring, not knowing.*

When I accept and honor the differences, I can recognize my partner as an independent being, not an extension of me or of my desires. Intellectually I have always known this. But now, in my bones and my heart, I see that my partner is another struggling human being. This is absolutely amazing! It should have been obvious, but my narcissism has kept me from seeing this simple truth. It is an astonishing revelation, because I thought that everything was about me.

She is not about me. She was not put in the world to take care of me. She is simply her own person, separate from me, working and laughing, fearing and celebrating, making the most she can of her life. Just like me. She hurts, she loves, sometimes she is foolish and at other times her vision is breathtakingly clear. Like me.

When at last I see this, I can stop expecting her to take care of me. I can master myself and (at least sometimes) offer her my love unencumbered by my ego. I can stop being dependent on our relationship and resenting it when I am disappointed. I can begin to enjoy our union in all its richness.

The epiphanal change for so many couples is this transition from criticism and competition to curiosity and acceptance. What is this person about? If she doesn't see it my way, then how does she see it? He sounds crazy to me; what is it about him that I don't understand?

So often our differences lead us into destructive ways of relating. Curiosity, empathy and personal responsibility engender acceptance, safety and intimacy.

Balancing the Boat

Picture a couple in a small sailboat. The boat tips a little to the right and the man leans out to the left to compensate. Fearing he leans too far, she cants to the right to provide balance. Alarmed that she will upset the boat, he moves further to the left... and so forth.

Complimentary traits can entangle, creating self-perpetuating cycles. She worries and he assures her that there is no problem. His bland optimism tells her that he isn't taking the situation seriously, and she worries more. As her anxiety mounts, he recounts all the sensible reasons not to worry. Feeling unheard, she experiences herself even more alone with the situation, until she is on the edge of panic. He thinks she's a tiresome worrywart; she thinks he's oblivious and unsupportive.

Another couple: she is an adventurous risk-taker, always ready to try the new and the unknown. Thinking her reckless, he inserts notes of caution, injecting into the conversation all the pitfalls he can think of. Impatient with his negativism, she plunges ahead while he becomes increasingly alarmed. The mutual exasperation mounts.

One more: in her loneliness, she repeatedly urges him to "express his deepest emotions". This is not in his repertoire; the last time he remembers deep emotion was when he hit his thumb with a hammer. Bewildered and feeling criticized, he withdraws further. She despises him as an emotional dullard; he tells his friends what a hysterical nag he married.

Yet these are the reasons they connected to begin with. He needs her passion and creativity; she needs his stability and practicality. Rather than thank each other, they engage in a contest over who is right and who is the better human being.

The contest may be loud and obvious or quiet and subterranean. In many marriages, one person is guilty of sins of silent omission while the other engages in sins that are easily seen. He is composed and phlegmatic as she escalates to heights of emotion; his passive provocation goes unnoticed while she is screaming with frustration. God help her, for everyone agrees that she's the crazy one.

Our job is to enter into relationship with these people in a way that allows them to rethink these differences, hopefully adopting a new paradigm for their relationship.

Briefly, a few of the ways we do this:

* Encouraging curiosity in place of judgment, acceptance in place of blame.
* Asking each partner to speak from his/her own experience, rather than assuming the motives of the other. It is the difference between "You did that to hurt me" and "I felt hurt"; between "You don't listen to me" and "I feel un-heard."
* Encouraging personal responsibility in place of victimhood. You may suffer by his behavior, and you can and should voice that. Now how do you contribute to the arrangement, and what can you do differently?
* Clean your own neighborhood. If you feel that your partner doesn't love you very much, find out what you can do to make yourself more lovable to him. Nagging and disparaging never gets you what you want.
* And most important: asking each partner to make his or her own changes. *You have no power to change what the other person does; but if you change what you do, you invite your partner to change.*

None of these adjustments are easy. Arlene and I had been in a couples' group for some time. One evening in the group we got to quarreling in a famil-iar, tiresome, but painful pattern. I tried to stop myself and use some of these new ideas, but my attempts fell short and our bickering continued. Then the group leader asked a question of us. I have no memory of the exact question, but I recall with sharp clarity the response it provoked in me. I stopped in my tracks and said to her in the presence of the group, "I see now what I'm doing. I've been trying to stop this by behaving differently, but when you don't respond immediately, I get resentful. I think, well I tried and you didn't appreciate it, so if you're not going to do your part, the hell with it. I see now that I have to keep doing my part whether or not you respond. So I'm going to try to do that, start-ing now."

With some coaching and practice I did it fairly well. The results were aston-ishing. Within days I sensed her responding in new ways, and I, in turn, re-sponded to her responses. This began a fresh cycle, one of accountability with ourselves and generosity with each other that has continued through the years.

Managing Conflict

The description that we used for intimacy is relevant here as well. *A healthy relationship is one in which each partner can be fully him/herself while being fully present with the other.* Because the partners are different, conflicting needs, tastes and desires are simply a fact of life.

Many of us have not learned to handle our conflicts in ways that serve the relationship. Instead we avoid them; we suppress personal differences, or we create enough physical or emotional distance so that those differences no longer matter. The disagreements can be driven underground in a sacrificial manner, or they can give rise to a pattern of resentment and guerrilla warfare. Other couples engage in open struggle, using criticism, intimidation, emotional blackmail, guilt, and verbal or physical violence. Or they may try to settle their differences in good faith and simply not know how to do that.

When couples suppress differences, there will be a region of numbness in the marriage. This deadness ends when they learn make it safe to come out in the open, and to tolerate the anxiety that goes with that. That may be in sharp contrast to what they have learned all their lives: good people don't get angry. Anger is wrong or invariably destructive. A good marriage is always a conciliatory one. And one's own needs must be continually sacrificed.

With maturity and practice, we can learn to minimize the wear and tear of conflict, settling differences in ways that leave both partners whole and the relationship undiminished. As a first step, it is helpful to understand the difference between anger and hostility. The word "hostile" comes from the Latin *hostis*, meaning an army, as in the Biblical word *host*. Hostility is the attempt to do what armies do—to damage, inflict pain or destroy. "Anger", on the other hand, comes from the Scandinavian *angst*, signifying anguish and longing. When I am angry with someone I love, I long to break through, to be heard, to re-join the person from whom I am momentarily estranged.

Like the weather, anger will simply occur. It is impossible to live closely with someone without ever being angry. Sometimes we are angry about a genuine offense; as time goes by, mistakes are made. Sometimes we have opposing needs. And often, we replay old events and expectations.

Hostility, on the other hand, is a choice. If we play victim, pretending to righteous innocence and blaming the other party, we choose hostility. When we seek ways to punish, retaliate or dominate, we are being hostile. But when we attend to our anger, trying to hear and be heard, mindful of our longing and willing to forgive, we are following a path of loving responsibility.

When couples fight destructively, we can explore the behavioral cycles that perpetuate the difficulties, discovering the (usually defensive) motives and needs behind the struggle. This opens the possibility of new understanding and new behaviors.

Grace and Michael have been a couple for eleven years. Much of that time has been tumultuous, for they have been unable to deal well with friction. Grace begins shouting when she is upset. Michael fretfully withdraws into sulking sarcasm. This leaves Grace overwhelmingly anxious, expecting some dreadful retaliation. Her anxiety turns to rage, she raises the volume, and they continue the cycle.

The therapist provides a new and disruptive feature in their relationship, accepting anger and conflict with equanimity and curiosity. Instead of just reacting, he invites them to say what they experience, to explore and articulate the meanings they attach to events. Now they can examine their reactions and begin to see how they provoke each other. It makes sense that Michael withdraws; he grew up with a mother who was always screaming with rage, accompanied by painful abuse of several sorts. Things were never peaceful, and Michael has always seen silence as safety and sarcasm as protection. As Grace's voice rises, Michael feels like a threatened and helpless child whose protection lies in mute retreat and subversive retaliation.

Grace, on the other hand, has reason for her anxiety. She grew up with a Greek father who wore his soul on the outside. He was loud and demonstrative and voiced his anger at some volume, but his laughter and his affection were equally boisterous. That was just his way, and Grace never found it threatening. Her mother, however, was contained and devious. She could turn without warning and sting like a scorpion. Grace never knew what to expect, so quiet times felt to her like walking a minefield. In Grace's mind, Michael's silence is a prologue to cruelty and betrayal, and his covert disrespect only heightens that fear.

Neither Michael's mother nor Grace's took responsibility for herself or her anger. Each behaved as if her discontents were the fault of others, and those others deserved punishment. Their children, now grown, cannot bear each other's anger without expecting treachery, grief and pain. Each reacts in ways that seem sensible to them but are dangerous in the eyes of the other.

As they come to understand each other's perceptual worlds, things begin to seem less dangerous. The image of the partner begins to separate from the image of the menacing mother. Rather than withdrawing, Michael practices telling Grace when he feels anxious or threatened, and this softens her anger and her voice. Instead of frantically anticipating his retaliation, she learns to wonder if he is afraid or hurt. A new cycle begins, one in which they learn to calm each other and manage conflict with interest and generosity.

A few basic axioms, in no particular order, about difference, anger and conflict:

* It's not always about you. When Tom loads the dishwasher, he takes all the items that Pam has already loaded and rearranges them. Pam feels criticized; he is showing her that she did it wrong. But Tom – a mechanical engineer – is simply compulsive about placing things in the most hydrodynamically efficient way. It has nothing to do with her. This understood, he is perfectly agreeable to her request that he take over loading the dishwasher.

* Anger is rarely a primary emotion. Once the person feels heard and responded to, it becomes possible to get to the emotions underlying the anger: fear, pain, sadness, deprivation, insecurity, helplessness and loneliness.

* There is no "objective truth" in a relationship. Couples fight about who said what and how, what happened exactly when, and why their actions are justified. This gets them absolutely nowhere. The exit from the dilemma is simply to accept the other's experience as being valid for them, whether or not you see it the same way. "Since you heard it that way, I can see why you would feel…"

* Everything that goes wrong is not someone's fault. Life is full of arbitrary events and painful tragedies. As the bumper sticker declares, *shit happens.*

* Everyone needs to be heard. No one needs to be criticized. Criticism provokes resentment and resistance; acceptance engenders safety, and may even invite change.

* Blame is easy. Empathy and recognition never go amiss.

* Loving relationships are not made up of marketplace transactions. Bargaining and keeping score precludes generosity and appreciation.

* I ask couples all the time: would you rather be right or be loved? Much of the time, you can't have both.

* A simple question that can lead the way out of many fights: What is it that you need from me right now?

Divorce

Joan Rivers tells us, "Half of all marriages end in divorce—and then there are the really unhappy ones." Unfortunately, there are some marriages that just should not continue.

There are many contributors to the erosion of a marriage. To name some of the common ones: unrealistic expectations, lack of relational skills, rigidity in the face of changing circumstances or the maturation of the partner, bad faith, arrogance and contempt, a runaway sense of entitlement, abuse of all sorts, and stubborn immaturity. Given good will, the disposition to learn and change, and sometimes a hand from the outside, most of these can be repaired. One exception: sometimes there has been damage over time that has crossed some invisible boundary of forgiveness that cannot be repaired.

There are two absolute prerequisites, without which difficulties are likely to be terminal. First, the partners must be similar in their beliefs about personal integrity and the proper treatment of others. If I feel strongly about honesty and see you as deceitful, I will not be able to honor or trust you. If you value people and I routinely behave disrespectfully or abusively, I will repeatedly offend, embarrass and alienate you.

Secondly, each partner must be willing to place the relationship among the highest priorities of his/her life. If the quality of the marriage is not near the top of each person's list, the couple will quickly be in trouble. If we place career or money first, or consistently put the children foremost, we allow our marriages to decay and become lifeless.

If these two conditions are met and both people are willing to work hard and to forgive, differences can be overcome. If they are not together on these two, nothing they do is likely to produce an enduring and satisfying relationship. Criticism becomes scorn, and defensiveness turns into stonewalling or flight. It is the end of the line, a dead relationship. For all sorts of reasons, some people choose to stay together anyway. At other times, our job as their therapist is to help effect the best possible separation.

At this point I tell people that there are two kinds of divorce: sad ones and hostile ones. For your own sake and that of your children, do everything you can to make this a sad one. There is a life-or-death difference, and too many people use the divorce process to punish the partner. An old Chinese proverb says, "When you go to get revenge, first dig two graves."

PART II: FAMILY THERAPY

What is Family?
All families are difficult at times. Some are disastrous. One thinks there ought to be a better way. It reminds me of Winston Churchill's statement about democratic government: "Democracy is the worst form of government ever invented. Except for everything else we've tried."

The quality of family life is critical for both children and adults. We thrive in families where there is love, acceptance, guidance, discipline and mutual respect.

A sane society promotes these qualities, doing what it can to support healthy family life. This requires attention to social issues on which we have done poorly, including education, healthcare and poverty. It also requires a broadminded definition of family.

Families vary remarkably from one another, not only in composition but also in culture. It is easy to be rigid and judgmental in our views of how things ought to be, but there is no simple set of "family values" that applies to everyone.

I grew up in the fifties, when we imagined that most families fit the putative "standard": two faithfully married, heterosexual parents, two or three children, and the ubiquitous dog named Spot. Mother took a subsidiary role and was contentedly domestic. Father knew best, was unfailingly patient and wise, and could solve any problem in thirty minutes (with breaks for commercials). The family was middle-class, white and tepidly Protestant, and no one ever raised their voice.

As a portrait of how most people lived, this was an illusion. It is still farther from reality in today's more open and pluralistic environment. Whether or not we like the changes, we must deal with the world as it is.

We can talk about the "average" family (thought even that isn't so average anymore), but we can no longer believe that we have a universal prescription for how families should be structured or how they should function. Or even what constitutes family.

In real-world terms, *today's family is a multigenerational group of people who consider themselves kin.* Many, if not most, are other than "standard." A few interesting numbers from the 2000 census: only 24% of American children live in nuclear families (down from 40% in 1970). While 70% of children reside in households where they are cared for by two adults, frequently those adults are not the two biological parents. Childrearing structures are non-traditional, with single parents, at-home fathers, working couples, gay parents, stepparents, adoptive parents, children raised by grandparents, and numerous other arrangements of varied descriptions. All these configurations of family can be healthy for the children, and all can be problematic and destructive.

In today's reality, the family is who the family says it is. Whatever the legalities, and whatever our preferences or religious beliefs, as therapists we are in no position to declare otherwise. They all need and deserve our support.

The Relational Ground of Family Therapy

Nowhere is our binocular vision more pertinent. We must be cognizant of both personal and interpersonal experience, shifting from one to the other as called for. Along with individual life situations, people bring all their encounters with each other, and all the assumptions, reactions, expectations and hopes bred of those experiences.

We begin by providing a safe place for the work. This family comes to your office because there are things they haven't been able to untangle on their own. There are many reasons for this, the most important being fear (lack of knowledge is a close second). The first task in family therapy is the establishment of safety. Until they have at least a minimal sense of security, they cannot risk doing with you what they cannot safely do at home.

In supervision group, Ellen tells us about the Jacksons. They have been seeing her weekly for months. They are lovely, bright people, but they are a family in disarray. It is easy to see that they truly care for each other, but anger and frustration fill the room, regularly culminating in one or another of the teenagers storming out. Those remaining sit wretchedly, once again experiencing humiliating failure. This scene, of course, echoes what happens at home. Ellen's attempts to teach them "communication and conflict resolution" are getting nowhere. It is not safe to continue what they have been doing, but trying anything new seems even more dangerous.

In the next family session after supervision, Ellen shares the frustration, asking them to help her create some conditions for change. With her guidance, they devise a set of procedures—rituals, really—that will give everyone a chance to be heard and taken into account. They agree that no one will walk out, but will use the new process to make their dissatisfactions known. Then they discuss how things will be handled when someone violates these new agreements, for someone surely will. Having established this new degree of safety, they are ready to begin addressing other difficulties.

A second foundational issue is that of blame. Many families arrive in our offices with issues of culpability high on their agendas. Each wishes to avoid being blamed, either by other family members or by the therapist. They attack, defend, accuse, justify, scapegoat, lie, argue their cases, and wage guerrilla warfare. They don't necessarily like doing these things; it is all they know to do. It is the therapist's purpose to show them other ways, to reframe and reinterpret, to set an example of listening, acceptance and respect, and to demonstrate the desire to understand rather than to judge and punish. She shows that this is not a zero-sum game, that there need not be losers.

Successful therapy requires looking into attitudes and assumptions about family relationships. I have a few axioms that I try to make clear:

Family life is about growth and development. Conflicting needs are an expected and natural part of that.

While we sometimes seem to be enemies, we are in fact in the same boat. We influence each other, depend on each other, and are in some ways responsible for each other. We don't win when someone else loses. No boat sails successfully by tossing some of its crew overboard.

This means that the boat itself is important, and so is everyone in it. Everyone needs and deserves to be heard, considered and accepted.

Families must find and re-find the balance between membership and individuation. There is no answer to be arrived at; it is always changing.

Most people are doing the best they know how. Few of us intend evil, but we all get confused and frightened, and screw up. This makes ongoing forgiveness an absolute necessity.

Forgiveness is not free; as all our religions tell us, it requires confession, repentance and change.

Consciousness is perhaps the most important element of deliberate family change. When we become conscious of our actions, intentions, and effects, we open the possibility of making new choices.

Adolescence is a ubiquitous occurrence that illustrates all these premises. These are sometimes spoken of as "the awful years." We expect them to be extravagantly painful for the adolescent and everyone around him. That's the myth. The truth is that adolescence is a time of enormous personal and familial change, and therefore challenging. It may be difficult, but it doesn't have to be a disaster.

There is a difference between life's difficulties and the problems we create. Difficulties are part of living, and some of them are unavoidable. My balding scalp is one of life's difficulties. I can choose to accept it, remembering that my worth does not lie in the thick dark hair I once had. If I spend money that I can't afford on drugs or transplants, I have created a problem. If I blame my hair loss on my wife's nagging and failure to appreciate me, I have *really* created a problem.

Adolescence is one of life's difficulties, for the young person and for his family. Everything is changing, and not just hormonally. There are the brand new issues of mobility, sex, alcohol and drugs, and unprecedented peer pressure. The parent is losing a child, having to adapt to a growing independent spirit that is neither child nor yet adult, adjusting to this new being who just won't remain dependent and compliant. The adolescent is stretching his wings, wanting independence and terrified of it at the same time (not that he'll ever let you know that). As he prepares for adulthood, his mother (most often) is being forcibly retired from her childrearing career, and her husband must adapt to *her* resurgence of personal needs and increasing independence. If this is a single-parent home, or one with other adults about, things can get even more complicated.

A useful map for navigating the difficulties of adolescence would be based not just on the psychology of the young person, but on a developmental family perspective as well. It would look something like this:

You (we tell our newly emerging adolescent) are no longer a child. You're beginning a long transition to adulthood, and that may not be easy for you or for us. Your job is gradually to take on more responsibility, and with that will go more freedom to make your own decisions. It will often be difficult to know what you are or are not prepared to handle. Most of the time you will think that you're ready for more freedom than we, the adults, think you are. That's not because you're being difficult or because we don't want you to have a life of your own; we will just have different priorities. You will want to protect your privacy and freedom, and we will want to protect *you*.

Often there won't be any clear answer, and we will just have to struggle with it. You will feel impatient with us and we will sometimes try to overprotect you. You will feel we are stifling you and we will feel rejected or scared when you don't do as we think you should. The best we can do is to muddle through together, and we will make mistakes. You won't always get what you want, but we'll try always to listen and to respect you.

The Therapist with Families

Much of what has been said about couples is applicable to therapy with families, most particularly the material on tasks, differences, and the management of conflict.

Here too, the therapist assumes a role in the family. He becomes privy to the most astonishing intimacies and family secrets. He is asked to buffer, to moderate, to judge, advise, teach and direct. And the sheer inertia of reciprocal behavior invites him to participate in the dynamics that brought them to his office in the first place. *One way of stating the essence of family therapy is that the therapist resists enlistment; we strive to be who we are in our relationship with them, rather than participating in their problematic ways of being.* This occurs, for example, when we fail to participate in scapegoating the "identified patient," or when we are quietly indifferent to rigid gender roles.

We have some ideas about what works and doesn't work in families, but we are careful about imposing our own prejudices. We are prepared to modify our thinking in the face of cultural, ethnic and individual variations.

Of course, the essential distinction from couple therapy is that we are dealing with two or more generations, and the families often include minor children. Adult partners can be treated as equals, or at least potential equals. But children are not adults, and a healthy multigenerational family is not a democracy. Children need to be empowered, but must not be given responsibilities beyond their developmental readiness.

Child rearing is not easy, and most of us have little preparation for it. Because of their own familial experiences, parents naturally approach it with some different ideas and inclinations. Commonly, one parent will pay more attention to the need for nurture while the other is more alert to issues of guidance and discipline. Each sees his or her part of the picture and tends to miss the other half. She accuses him of being too lax, letting the kids take advantage of him. He dislikes her severity and inflexibility. When he is able to learn more firmness from her and she learns more adaptability from him, they become an effective team. They support each another, to the child's relief. Kids need consistency as much as they need to be cherished; much family therapy is really couple therapy with the responsible adults. As they work out their differences, learning respect and cooperation, they become more capable and loving parents.

A key task for the family therapist is the shifting of attention from concrete issues to relational processes. The Jacobs' household is in frequent turmoil, revolving about the fulminating anger between Father and his 17-year-old son Richard. A recurring theme concerns Richard's use of the family car.

If the therapist focuses on the subject matter of their arguments, she might get them to work out compromises about the car—and later wonder why no one sticks to the agreements. Instead, she explores how each of them responds to his understanding of their relationship.

It emerges that when Father says no, Richard hears him as withholding and controlling. Inarticulate about his anguish, he angrily insists on taking the car, and enlists his mother in the fight. Father, feeling challenged and manipulated, becomes sullen and stubborn; that in turn confirms Richard's sense of rejection.

As the therapist helps them articulate their needs and understand each other's perceptions, there is a shift. Eventually Father is able to tell Richard about his uneasiness and his anxiety as he watches Richard step out into the world. He needs to see himself as a competent and protective father, as his father was not. Richard finally discloses his yearning for Father's acceptance and approval. The entire level of discourse softens. It's no longer about the car, but about whom they are to each other. Continuing the automotive metaphor, the therapist suggests that they watch the curve in the road, and not get trapped arguing about the sign that says Curve Ahead.

As therapists to families, we give intense and continual attention to relational processes, and to moving the dialogue to a metalevel of feeling, motivation and understanding. We must call people's attention to the road, not the road sign.

CHAPTER 12
ALTERNATE ROUTES AND DETOURS

Group Therapy

Professor Limentani specialized in group therapy with hospitalized psychotic patients. In response to my question, he defined a group as "a gathering of two or more people, at least one of whom is actually there."

Many therapists meet with groups of all descriptions. But much of what is called group therapy merely focuses on one member and then another. It is not truly group work, but revolving individual therapy with the group as audience.

Aside from allocation of resources, the great advantage of group therapy is its function as a living relationship laboratory. Even in a small group, the permutations of relationships are nearly unlimited. As in individual and family therapy, we bring into the group all our past and present relationships, replicating them in many ways. We play out behaviors and assume characteristics that mirror our roles with family, friends and others. This occurs in full view in an environment that encourages immediate and direct feedback. It affords us the opportunity for new perspectives on our ways of relating, comparing our expectations and preconceptions with the immediate reality of the group.

Eddie, a twenty-year-old still living with his parents and holding only an occasional job, is adept at provoking uneasiness within the group. He makes critical and vaguely threatening remarks, and when asked to explain, changes the subject or goes silent. The others are left feeling anxious, defensive and frustrated; soon these emotions boil over, driving dissention and conflict in the group. Eddie quietly observes.

After a few episodes, others become aware of the pattern, and they are not happy about it. Because the group is encouraged to honesty and directness, Eddie now hears varying reactions to his behavior. Someone expresses helpless frustration, another speaks of feeling used, and several are angry. He is confronted with the anguish that people experience over his lack of responsibility and his willingness to set others at odds.

Not surprisingly, this replicates events at home. When his parents try to talk with him about getting on with his life, their unending conflicts over him intensify and their disagreements turn bitter. While they pummel each other, Eddie slips off unnoticed.

This wily behavior "works" in his family. It allows him to continue his life unchanged, and it may serve some real or imagined function in his parents' marriage. When the group members disrupt the cycle by responding in ways unlike his parents, Eddie hears directly the effects of his behavior; he can't avoid the feelings directed at him. He begins to understand that what he does precludes the belonging and acceptance he so desperately wants.

The group provides each member the opportunity to see how he invites people to relate to him: with acceptance or avoidance, closeness or distance, anger or warmth, wariness or trust. Eddie can no longer imagine that he is just a victim; he is shown to be an active agent in the way others treat him.

In the group we replicate our typical roles in life: rescuer, scapegoat, caretaker, leader, passive observer, intimidator and so forth. All our usual relational arrangements are repeated in this environment.

Change is possible because the culture of the therapy group is different from that of our daily lives. In a well-functioning group high value is placed on caring, directness, the building of trust, honesty with oneself and others, generosity of spirit, the willingness to learn, and acceptance of individuality and diversity.

Individual and relational issues will come to the fore. But it is a mistake to allow too much exploration of just one member's issues at a given time; the therapist then leads the group in what is essentially individual therapy with spectators. In the most effective groups, the group itself does most of the therapy. Our job is that of leader, primarily attending to two functions.

The first task of the group leader is to create and maintain the culture that makes therapy possible. Group norms must promote emotional and physical safety; this includes trust, responsibility, inclusion, cohesion, confidentiality, expectations of attendance and dependability, and the management of conflict, anger and authority.

In general, rule making by the therapist is an ineffective way of creating this culture. The therapist must lead, but only the group itself can successfully establish and maintain its own mores. To take a common example, we know that subgrouping can be destructive to the group as a whole, so therapists frequently decree that members not gather outside the designated time and place. But—as with drugs or sex—prohibition seldom stops the behavior; it simply drives it underground, creating secret alliances and covert activities that become sources of group subversion.

Instead of mandating a rule, the therapist might explain that research and experience has shown secret alliances to be destructive to the group, and these connections are commonly formed when members meet outside and without the group's knowledge. She can then ask people how they wish to handle this issue. If they want to simply prohibit such meetings, she can raise the question of managing violations. Another possibility—one that I prefer—is to ask people not to sabotage the therapy; they can agree that if outside meetings do occur, the people involved will report back on their encounter and any subsequent relationships that are formed. Even an intramural romantic relationship need not endanger the therapy if it can be discussed openly.

The principle is to avoid secrets, and to give everyone a stake in preserving the functioning and the code of conduct of the group.

In our treatment center for drug addicts, many of our patients came to us directly from the street life, and many had done time. High-level anger, even to the point of rage, was a daily occurrence in group meetings, and violence could be a real threat. Understanding that such behavior would make treatment impossible, and could even destroy the facility, the patients and staff agreed on a simple rule: while verbal expressions of anger were to be unrestricted, no one would leave his seat. Occasionally someone—agitated and forgetting himself—would leap up yelling or make threatening gestures. Fifteen people instantly turned on him and shouted, "Sit down!" There was never a time that this wasn't effective.

The group leader's second principal task is to call attention to relational processes. If people are in conflict, the therapist's attention will be only secondarily on the content; his first interest will be in *how* people disagree. Is someone being provocative, or passive-aggressive, or intimidating? Is she belligerent, conciliatory, deferential, respectful or seductive? How do other people feel about what is going on? What does it arouse for them? Does one person tend to speak for the group, and how do the others allow that to happen? Who habitually acts as provocateur, and who plays the role of peacemaker? How do others respond and what does that say to them? If people disagree with the therapist, do they feel safe to voice it? If not, is it something about the therapist's behavior or do they bring authority issues into group with them, or both?

Group work can be an exciting and extraordinarily powerful way of doing therapy. It provides abundant and recurring opportunities to examine relationships "live", and to try out new ways of being and of being with others.

Brief Psychotherapy

Also spoken of as short-term, time-limited, and focused psychotherapy, brief therapy is a subject of ideological, economic, theoretical and pragmatic controversy. I'll not attempt to settle all of that, but a few observations might be in order.

First off, the reality is that we all do brief therapy, though we don't always do it on purpose. Some therapy should be brief because it's all that people need. This is particularly true when a counseling approach is called for, or when a small shift in perspective can free a large capacity for growth, as is frequently the case with young people.

In some cases, time and changing circumstances relieve the pressure and the anxiety, and the client loses interest. Or she may be satisfied with her initial gains and wish to go no further. We may disagree with her reasons (for example, she doesn't want to address certain issues that we think are important). We can and should offer our views, especially if we think she may be leaving herself vulnerable to further difficulties, but the decision isn't ours. Often she lets us know that she's finished for now by simply stopping without consulting us.

Brief therapy has some real advantages, not the least of which is economic. In a public service facility it may represent the very best allocation of limited resources. This is true also in a private arrangement where payment for more extended therapy poses a significant burden. It may be that time is limited by circumstances; how can this student and I best meet her needs in the weeks before she heads back to college? These are necessary and appropriate concessions to the world's reality.

But I take a moment to rant: *The first consideration in each of these cases must be the welfare of our clients, not the prosperity of a third-party payer.* The subordination of therapeutic decisions to considerations of corporate profit is an abomination that should not be tolerated by any principled society. The ideals of our profession demand that we do everything we can to resist it.

Brief therapy poses other advantages. It may simply fit the client's disposition or values, his capacity and desire for change, or the fragility of his personality. Sometimes it serves as a prelude to longer-term therapy, either at the time or later when he returns for more work.

On the other hand, much important and demanding treatment cannot be accomplished in a brief setting. Many people have a desire and a need for extensive transformation. The magnitude and complexity of issues, along with the difficulty of changing long-standing ways of perceiving and functioning, may require time and repetition. Some issues simply have to be developed gradually and patiently. Most importantly, *there is a level of intimacy, comfort and trust that can be developed only through time and repeated reinforcing of the alliance.* Without that, many topics will never be broached, let alone achieve a degree of resolution.

One significant negative does not concern brief therapy itself, but the way in which it is too often taught. Many approaches are exceedingly directive, technique-oriented, and/or superficial, based on oddly oversimplified notions of human nature. Bear in mind that good short-term therapy is still relational, still psychodynamic, still binocular in its viewpoint. It cannot be prescriptive. It will usually have a focus of attention but not a stipulated goal, and it does not presume that the therapist knows exactly what is good for the client. It is not an accident that most therapists who are best at brief psychotherapy are those who are already accomplished at long-term therapy.

The Media Guru

Two very differing premises permeate our media, our politics, and our society in general. The first is a culture of victimhood, a mentality that says—against all evidence of reality—that *things don't just happen.* Bad events are someone's fault; we have been deliberately or negligently injured, and we deserve to be rescued, compensated or revenged. It is this cast of mind that gives rise to a litigious society: someone has done me wrong, and that someone must pay.

The other, and contradictory, theme presents the image of decisive do-it-all-by-yourself individualism. Contrary as these are—victimhood and hypercompetent individualism—the success of mass media "therapists" is fueled by both premises. We would all love to be rescued by a powerful and wise parent, one who has the answers and is never in doubt. At the very same time we may feel revulsion over all the foolish whining and blaming we hear, and the guru expresses this for us. We, too, sometimes want to say, "Cut the crap! Get real!" We are certain that if we were in the plaintiff's predicament, we would have behaved much better.

The suppliant, borne witness by the entire media audience, brings his predicament before the master. The problem is immediately redefined in the guru's terms, which may or may not be compatible with the petitioner's experience. The guru has little patience but lots of solutions, and these solutions carry the implication that the individual is (at least slightly) defective. You've been inadequate; just do what I tell you and everything will be all right.

We are presented with "common sense" resolutions that deny the need for specialized knowledge, patience or hard thought. This media event is no more typical of psychotherapy than talk radio's rantings represent real political thought: both are entertainment, full of slogans, highly satisfying to our desire for simplification. In real life the work of creating substantive change begins *after* the advice is given, after the petitioner receives his marching orders and can't carry them out. Advice remains cheap.

The guru's responses are always about answers, always about what to do. They are rarely about compassion, thoughtfulness, resilience or courage. They assure us that life's difficulties can be reduced to simple formulations, and all have solutions, if you'd just use your head!

Self-help

My two-year-old was testing new capabilities, exerting her independence. She resisted my offer of help, saying, "Do it self!"

The term "self-help" is used in at least two distinct ways. The first of these, very much a part of pop culture, refers to the lone individual. In this meaning of self-help, you can learn what you need to know by reading a book, hearing a lecture, attending a seminar or just being clever. You don't require support. You don't need to ask for help. You can do everything you need to do without ever having to enter into a relationship with anyone.

This assumes that life's lessons are all written down somewhere. The right book or workshop will tell you how you have been co-dependent, love-addicted, abuse surviving, disempowered, or whatever this season's hot topic is. Then it will give you an eight-point program for overcoming it, while also quitting smoking and losing thirty pounds.

Many of these books are shallow or gimmicky or both. A small number are useful. Some will give you helpful things to think about, especially if you don't take labels too seriously. It is certainly nice to relieve one's sense of isolation: "You mean I'm not the only person who faces this problem?" No, you're not the only man who wants several incompatible things at once, the only woman to be baffled by relationships, the only person to feel confused and helpless; you're not alone in questioning your sexuality, your parenting, or your capacity for love.

Some of the better books can serve educational and even counseling functions. Just don't confuse that with the processes of personal change; there will be no caring presence, no connection, no intuitive understanding. Books cannot be therapeutic; therapy takes place in a relationship.

Addressing life in all its messiness, uncertainty and unpredictability requires patience, integrity and determination. It takes fortitude to accept complexity and ambiguity. It calls for personal connection, relatedness, and frequently community. Life does not come with an instruction manual; it needs much more than a set of "skills".

These books cannot be personal. Unless you are one of a tiny group of people that includes Mahatma Gandhi, Albert Einstein and Eleanor Roosevelt, no one has written a book about *you*.

The writers of these books are not living your life. Your own therapist frequently does not know what is right for you, so why would you trust some anonymous author? The writers of instructional books (including this one) are working from their own perspective and experience, which may or may not be relevant for you. And many of them are rank amateurs.

I often think that self-help books are most useful precisely to people who don't really need them, but may not know that yet.

Support Groups

In this very different version of self-help, the central idea is one of community, a cooperative effort among people dealing with a set of shared difficulties. Used in this manner, *self* indicates that people can assist and nurture each other in many ways, rather than relying entirely on professionals. This is the basis for support groups of all kinds. The term *mutual help* might be more accurate.

The most outstanding and effective example is Alcoholics Anonymous, along with other twelve-step programs patterned on it. Their first principle is that you cannot overcome all your difficulties by yourself; the Lone Ranger is not a member of this group.

No quick or easy solutions are offered. Instead, AA advocates a series of carefully thought-out steps to be worked on "one day at a time" for a lifetime. There is heavy emphasis on spiritual values and on social and personal support. The individual learns to depend on sharing, commitment, frequent contact, and serious introspection and personal responsibility. It offers life-lessons, the most striking of which is its frequently-invoked Serenity Prayer: "God grant me the serenity to accept the things I cannot change; the courage to change the things I can; and the wisdom to know the difference." This is a discernment we all need to practice.

Alcoholics Anonymous is not only the most effective treatment for alcoholism and other addictions; it is also a program for living that could benefit anyone. We would do well to get together and establish People Anonymous.

Of course, no approach—twelve-step, psychotherapy, religion or anything else—offers all the answers for everyone. For our purposes, the combination of psychotherapy and a twelve-step program can create a powerful ecology for transformation. I often encourage my clients to participate in AA, Alanon, and similar groups, and I don't hesitate to borrow ideas and language from the program. This business of life-change is difficult; let's use every instrument we have.

Ideological Counseling

I received an announcement for the opening of a new therapy clinic "specializing in Christian Counseling". I was curious. The term suggested clergy providing guidance to people on matters of faith; I hadn't heard it in the context of mental health. Were they simply saying that their therapy was shaped by their faith and their ethics, or was there more to it?

I was acquainted with one of the therapists on the staff, so I called to ask him what exactly "Christian Counseling" meant. He told me, "We believe that in order to achieve mental health, a person has to get in proper relationship with Jesus Christ." I thanked him and ended the conversation, resolved that I would never refer anyone to this group.

Certainly I have no problem with someone getting into good relationship with Jesus Christ, or with whatever manifestation of the divine is meaningful to him. As I will argue later, we have a legitimate role in helping some people discover their own spiritual directions. But promoting a particular theology, or imposing one as a criterion of mental health, is a distortion of the therapeutic endeavor. It can also pitch us into noxious battles over whose version of religion, or of God, is "mentally healthy".

Religion is not the only culprit here. Other ideologies—dogmatic Marxism, doctrinaire (as opposed to thoughtful) feminism, even psychoanalytic orthodoxy—have been similarly misused. All have insights to offer. Any of them may inform our practices. They must not be allowed to subvert the definition and direction of the healing endeavor.

The proper focus of psychotherapy is the discovery and actualization of the individual and the enabling of intimate and loving relationships. Psychotherapy driven by ideology is no longer psychotherapy. Religious guidance and persuasion have an important place in life; when they intrude into therapy, they undermine its purposes. Fostering an ideology in the name of mental health tells people what they must believe and who they must be, even at the expense of their own experience.

Certainly, everything that is enlightening is not therapy. Our spiritual practices and our other relationships, for example, may well be growth producing. Therapy is about healing wounds and removing the obstacles to that growth.

Co-Therapy

Co-therapy is the engagement of two or more therapists in a given therapy situation. Other than its use for training purposes, it is rarely helpful or economical when applied to a single client. It has its uses in family and group therapy. It can provide perspective, lighten the workload, add a pair of ears and a voice, and help remobilize stuck situations.

But its most powerful contribution occurs when we pay attention to the relationship of the therapists.

Dee and William are seeing a couple together. As Dee is pursuing a line of thought with them, William seems to change the subject. Dee feels irritated and discounted. She uses her feelings as cues to the situation, first expressing her annoyance courteously but directly to William. She asks the woman if her husband often changes the subject on *her*, what does she do when that happens, and what follows? William listens respectfully and he and Dee work through this difficult moment together. It provides the couple with a model for handling their own conflicts.

Lily and I lead a group together. It has been a rough evening, with people contentious and divided into sub-groups. One side identifies the other as rigid, and in turn is accused of irresponsibility. I can't sort it out. After a while I realize I'm feeling crabby and defensive, and I'm not sure why.

Then I realize that my testiness is aimed in Lily's direction, and I've been short with her. We have a warm relationship, and normally enjoy each other's company. One reason we work well together is that our inclinations balance each other nicely: she is methodical and thorough, while I often engage in unsystematic leaps of intuition.

So... yep, the group has got us. Half of them are lined up on the side of intuition, the other half on circumspection. They're fighting over whether Mom or Dad is taking better care of them. I am feeling cranky with Lily because "her" group is chastising me for being reckless, while "my" group is reproving her for being overly cautious. In front of the group, I share this perception with Lily, who admits that she's found me irritating tonight. The discussion to which this leads becomes a turning point in the life of the group, raising issues of personal style, parenting and sibling rivalry, among others.

Relationships are contagious. What happens between the therapists is more often than not what is happening within the couple, the family or the group.

CHAPTER 13
PERENNIAL CONCERNS

A number of difficult topics arise continually in practice and in supervision. In many cases there are standardized responses. In many cases these responses miss the point. They do so because the relational context is omitted.

Suicide

The client's self-destruction is a threat that every therapist must sooner or later confront. Faced with this possibility, we feel frightened and unnerved. We fear for the client, it threatens our sense of competence, and we worry about our work and our reputation. On all levels, we devoutly hope that this risk does not become a reality.

We look desperately for resolutions. We hospitalize people; occasionally this makes sense, but often it is a reaction to our own panic, overlooking opportunities for clients and families to successfully negotiate crises. We call in the psychiatrist, hoping he has some magic to change things. We extract promises and "contracts", as though we can hold the client accountable if she chooses not to honor them.

While there are procedural moves that are often helpful—frequent contact, medication, mobilizing the family—we must not underestimate the role of our presence and caring. The suicidal client is desperate for a bond, a sense that she belongs somewhere, an indication that her existence counts. Any sense of hope, patience or restraint that we can offer will occur in the contest of our relationship with her.

This must be honestly personal as well as professional.

Client: No one will care if I'm gone.

Therapist: I will. I'll be very unhappy if you kill yourself.

Client: You'll get over it.

Therapist: I'll go on, but it will hurt like hell and I'll really miss you.

Client: It matters to you?
Therapist: You matter to me.
Holding the client in caring relationship is the best anti-suicide measure we have. We do well not to let our anxiety make us forget this.

Anger

Anger is a frequent and important event in psychotherapy. It may be emergent in the client's life, it may be directed at us, or both. It may be transferential or existential. If we handle it well, it offers opportunity.

The first thing the angry person needs is to know he is heard. Then he needs a validating response.

"Let me be sure I understand you. When you began telling me about your sister, I went on with something else, and that felt dismissive of your feelings. Of course you felt angry; no one likes to be discounted. I apologize for that. I didn't mean any disrespect; I just missed how important it was. Can we talk about it now?"

Anger is almost always a secondary emotion. Once the individual feels heard and taken to heart, we can get to the underlying feelings. Most commonly, anger is a way of making oneself less vulnerable to the "softer" emotions of sadness, helplessness, fear, pain, rejection or disappointment; dealing with these feelings is key to one's further healing.

It helps to recognize the difference between anger and hostility. Hostility is an assault, an attempt to damage, to inflict pain, to control or destroy. When we seek ways to punish, retaliate or dominate, we are indulging in hostility.

Anger, by contrast, is a reaching out. It arises from anguish, longing and vulnerability. In my anger I long to break through, to be heard, to somehow remedy the situation, perhaps to re-join the person from whom I am momentarily estranged. *Anger is a natural occurrence, while hostility is a choice.*

When we attend responsibly to our anger, trying to hear and be heard, we are following a path of caring and return.

Violence

It is a small office in a clinic, barely large enough for the two of us. Gerry is agitated, and it makes me uneasy; he has a history of violence, and he's a big guy.

"Gerry, I need your help with a problem. I see you're angry, and we should talk about that. But I know you've lost it in the past, and I don't want to be attacked. We can work this out, but I don't do that very well when I'm afraid. I know you don't want to hurt me. Do you think you can be in control right now, or do we need to find a way to cool things down?" I make it *our* problem, instead of his or mine.

He isn't sure. Opening the door to the office, I tell him again that it's not his anger I mind, and we will talk about it as much as we need to; but first I want to make it safe for both of us. We agree that he will take a walk around the building and come back before the hour ends.

When he returns, I thank him for working on this with me. We make another appointment and agree that our leading agenda will be to talk about what
happened today.

I have first of all assured my own safety. Ignoring my fear would not do.
Nor would bravado, nor would a counter threat.

Beyond that, I have given him several important messages. That I am vulnerable but I believe in his goodwill toward me. That we can work conjointly to
create safety; *today has been a success, not a failure.* We did that together. His
anger needn't be dangerous and there are ways to work out difficulties; our relationship can continue.

Grief

This is one of the toughest. It's daunting because *there is nothing to do.*
There are no therapeutic interventions, no helpful homilies, no treatment plans
or goals, no way to make things better.

I sit with Ellen and Mark as they mourn the death of their twenty-year-old
son. We have been doing this for several months now. It is a dreadful loss, beyond expression, almost beyond comprehension.

Why do they keep coming to see me? There is nothing I can do to change
things; I have no way to relieve their pain.

I have only one thing to offer; but that one thing is precious to them and to
me. I am fully here with them; I open myself to their anguish, their horror, their
fear and their rage. I understand how angry they are with God, and that God accepts that. I feel their utter helplessness, their sensation of failure as parents. I
am brutally aware of mortality, of vulnerability, of the terror of experiencing a
similar loss in my life. I weep with them.

Why would I choose to do this? Why put myself through it with them, again
and again? For the honor of being connected with them in their courage and en-
durance, and for the sake of being alive in the face of loss and death. And also
because it is the only thing that can help. What we can offer so often depends on
how much we are willing to endure.

The Unlikable Client

Most of our clients—indeed most people—are not difficult to care about.
But some are, and we all know a few.

Some are cranky, negative, and occasionally hostile. They invite displeas-
ure, rejection, even retaliation. We must remember that this individual's behavior in therapy reflects his behavior in the rest of life. It has served some function,
however maladaptive or self-defeating. *When we look for the pain behind the
unpleasantness, we are likely to discover the wounded person with whom we can
successfully relate.*

We may react irritably to the client who represents our own shadow side. If
I struggle with impulses to wander from my marriage, it can appear in subtle
ways with my adulterous client. If telling the truth has been an issue for me, the
client who lies will invite my disapproving projections.

Sometimes we are troubled by something in the client's way of relating to us. Megan is a recovering drug addict who is seeing me while completing the outpatient portion of her recovery program. I realize that I don't look forward to her sessions; I feel somehow used. The impasse isn't broken until I confront her about my lack of trust. This precipitates a stormy exchange that finally clears the air; Megan admits that she has been keeping from me information about her behavior, fearing that I won't help her get back her pharmacist's license.

We like people with whom we can feel successful. We become frustrated with clients that don't change. For their part they may not be ready to move, or they may be too frightened, or change presents them with too much to lose: if I stop this pattern in my marriage, he may leave me. Some people need support more than change.

In these situations we are easily disappointed, and we find ourselves thinking that this is an undesirable client; we may even give him a pejorative label like "borderline" or "manipulative". We do well to remember that our task is investigating and facilitating change, not driving it; it isn't our decision, since we will not live with the consequences of that change. If we provide the environment that enables it, we have done our job.

Even when we see beyond these difficulties, utilizing our own resources and those of our supervisors and peers, we still sometimes find ourselves lacking empathy. Nothing we do works; perhaps we are just worn out. It is time to make a referral.

The referral should be an honest one that does not blame the client. The therapist to whom we refer must know of our difficulties in the situation. The client must understand that we consider this an unproductive pairing, not a defect on his part. Referral will give him a fresh start unencumbered by our history.

Addiction

There are essentially four choices available in confronting life's pain. We can face it with stoic acceptance. We can wallow in it, enjoying the delicious satisfaction of being a victim. We can find a way to transmute pain into meaning. Or we can narcotize it. The last of these constitutes our most popular choice, and it is the basis for addiction.

Addiction is a complex subject. In all the complexity, we'd best not lose sight of the relational context.

I was attending the treatment planning meeting at a small rehab hospital to which I sometimes referred people. The staff had been compiling follow-up data, and informed me that a substantially greater than average percentage of my alcoholic patients finished the program and remained sober afterwards. We agreed that the main reason was my insistence on engaging the families in the treatment from the beginning.

We need not belabor the point. Instead, I want to discuss some difficulties with our idea of what constitutes addiction. This may be the single most misunderstood area we work in, for at least two reasons.

To begin, all compulsive behavior is not addiction. *Stedman's Medical Dictionary* defines addiction as "habitual psychological and physical dependence on a substance, that is beyond voluntary control (sic)." This is a precise and useful definition of addiction, even if it's not very good syntax. It tells us that addictions have to do not only with compulsive behavior but also with substance abuse, emotional numbing, psychological and physical dependence, physiologic craving and drug withdrawal.

Over the last two decades the word "addiction" has been appropriated to cover a huge range of compulsive or repetitive behaviors, as diverse as gambling, shopping, overeating, engaging in bouts of rage, risk-taking, sexual adventurism, physical exercise and even (I'm not making this up) the use of profanity. It almost seems that anything done more than twice is an addiction.

This sort of thinking has its uses, particularly in the self-help movement. The most spectacularly successful treatment for true addiction is found in the twelve-step spiritual journey embodied in Alcoholics Anonymous. That twelve-step program has been appropriated to treat all sorts of habitual and compulsive behavior, even when the model is a poor fit. By calling something an addiction we can borrow the program wholesale and tell ourselves we have both a clearly defined problem and a solution. If it doesn't apply, we stretch it and distort it until it does.

People do things obsessively, yet we don't think of a person with an obsessive condition as being "addicted" to checking locks, washing hands or counting the cracks in the sidewalk. These behaviors are obsessive and compulsive, and we have long sought ways to treat that. It is of dubious value to label all these folks "addicts", and it may leave us with the illusion that we have simple explanations and solutions for mysterious and complex human difficulties.

We can also draw a distinction between addiction and habit: when a habit begins to cause you harm, you can stop it.

Secondly, and importantly in our daily practice, *we must differentiate between medication use and drug abuse.* The fact that someone is medically, or even physiologically, dependent on a drug does not make that person an addict. When I wish to see clearly, I am dependent on my eyeglasses. No one accuses a diabetic of being addicted to insulin, or a heart patient of using digitalis to avoid life's struggles. Many patients treated with opiates for pain can simply be detoxified once their pain is relieved by other means. In the case of the true addict, detoxification is the easy part; the hard part is *staying* off drugs. Addiction is far more a psychological than a pharmacological condition.

Addiction is characterized by behavior more than by ingestion of a chemical. This behavior generally includes secretiveness, the obtaining of substances from multiple or illegitimate sources, escalating doses, deterioration of family and work life, and numbness or distortion of one's mental and emotional state. Relationally, the addict tends to be self-absorbed or absent.

There is also a difference in expectation, in the fantasized outcome. Gene relates the daydream that he harbored in his years on the street: he is lying in bed with a needle in his arm, the tubing attached to an infinitely large vat of liquid heroin dripping into his vein forever. There is no more pain, fear or struggle, only a numb and vaguely pleasant oblivion.

Medication enables one to cope better with the struggles of living. Addiction is driven by the whispered mendacious promise that all will be well forever.

Thinking about Sex

If you ever doubt the importance of sex in motivating human affairs, browse the world's libraries and museums. Then come back and tell us how much of our literature, science, politics and art has been produced by eunuchs. All none of it.

Clients often hesitate to raise the subject of sex in therapy; they don't know how to talk about it, or even if they may. They frequently need us to take the initiative and to be available and reasonably comfortable with the subject. To do that, we must clear our minds as best we can of preconceptions and prejudices.

Our public attitudes are ambivalent at best. Even the supposed norm—heterosexual and relational sex—may be portrayed in a joyless way that suggests only grudging acceptance. Sometimes we try to present sexual love in a more positive light, but seldom does the media or public discussion celebrate (not *smirk about*) sex that is lusty, uninhibited and life-affirming.

The mere discussion of sexual appetite may be difficult. Some of sexuality's capacity to disturb us so deeply resides in its ability to take so many forms, display such variety and be so stubbornly uncontrollable. Mention masturbation, prostitution, homosexuality, sadomasochism or multi-partner sex, and you have pushed hot buttons across the community. Each of these activities is everyday practice for millions of people, but we find it painful and embarrassing even to name them. *As therapists, we must begin with human nature as it is, not as someone would like it to be.*

When I began seeing clients, I was astounded at how much sexual "deviance" I was encountering. With the guidance of my supervisors plus a lot of reading, I quickly came to understand that it wasn't deviance at all; I was simply meeting the real world of human sexual behavior. The difficulty was my own ignorance.

I was hardly alone. There is a deep silence regarding the extraordinary range of real-world sexuality. The most remarkable assumption is that there is a "right" or "natural" way, while other ways are abnormal, perverted, unnatural and ungodly.

The lives and stories of the people I've encountered over the years have taught me that *there is no such thing as "normal" or "abnormal" sexual inclination and behavior.* There is only a vast spectrum of impulse, desire and pleasure. The practices I've just mentioned bear testimony to our varied and untidy sexuality. Sexual behavior and even inclination can change over time. Fantasy is endless and creativity unlimited. We have the capacity for far greater variation in our sex lives than most of us desire or have the nerve to live out. *There cannot be any sexual "deviance" because there is no norm from which to deviate. The idea of "perversion" is difficult to defend when there is no standard behavior to pervert.*

"What, no norm?" we might protest. "When so many adults live in heterosexual marriages? Wouldn't that be the norm?"

Well, yes and no. It's true as a statistical statement. But statistics don't tell us about joy, quality, esthetics, imagination or obsession. Just look at the varied sexuality that exists even in monogamous heterosexual marriages. Karen and Bill, married sixteen years, occasionally enjoy having sex in semi-public places where there is a small chance of being caught. Larry and Stephanie have lost interest in sex, though they are only in their forties. Leslie likes sex but insists her husband wear condoms because semen is "dirty." One couple almost always has oral sex, another never does. Many couples enjoy watching pornography together while others find it distasteful. Leah likes ropes and handcuffs. Jerry and Paige dress in costumes. Sara and Arnold enjoy the use of a large collection of rubber and leather toys. Some like rough sex. Many couples like complete nudity while others prefer lingerie, garters and gimmicks. Max gets aroused when Carla urinates on his bare stomach. Tom is obsessed with cunnilinguis, to Tammy's delight. Jeannie likes to wear stockings and stiletto heels for lovemaking with her husband. And many, many people have enjoyable sex lives with their partners while entertaining (and sometimes sharing) fantasies of other people and strange situations.

This list doesn't even touch on all the voyeuristic and autoerotic things that married individuals do on their own, and which have no effect at all on their marriages.

The limitless field of sexual desire, preference and behavior defies categorization. It is multi-dimensional and cannot be contained in neat compartments. It defies the reality of appetite and experience to think, for example, that people are simply either heterosexual or homosexual, or even to imagine that the words "latent" and "bisexual" can fill the gaps. How would we categorize the lesbian who genuinely enjoys sex with a man if he acts out a game in which she plays the whore and he pays her five dollars? What of the married woman who finds her greatest excitement when she has sex with her husband and another woman?

Or the life-long gay male who discovers his capacity for erotic desire with a woman, as long as the woman is of a different race than his? I'm not making up these stories; these are all folks I've known.

And we think we can say what is "normal"?

Many people in the "sexually deviant" community, faced with the living inadequacy of definitions, have cast them aside and appropriated the word queer to describe themselves. Perhaps the real point of this... is that we are all queer.

"But what do I do," you may ask, "if I have prejudices or emotional reactions to gays (or sado-masochists or anyone else) that I can't seem to change?" This is a fair question. You may not be able to change your feelings or your reactions, and no one has a right to judge you for them. Growing up in our society, we are all touched by racial, sexual and other bigotry.

I was challenged about bigotry in a community mental health meeting. Most of the people at the conference table were African-American, including my boss. I had made some comment about the effects of racial discomfort on a project under discussion. One of the men looked at me sharply and said, "You mean to tell me you have no prejudices?" I thought for a moment, for he deserved a straight answer. Then I said to him, "I grew up in this country. I do have some reflexive prejudices. But I promise you something: I'll look you in the eye and try to find out who you are." The more one does this, the more prejudices and preconceptions soften.

When you find prejudices stirring, I suggest you own these reactions as a part of you. Don't project them onto other people as if there is something wrong with them for being who they are. Remember that this is *your* issue, not theirs. If you claim these fears and dislikes as part of your emotional property, then you recognize that they are personal. They are not laws of the universe. They call for no action. Simply taking responsibility for your individual responses does a great deal to diminish their power over you.

Sex and the Psychotherapist

Nowhere does the power differential of the psychotherapy relationship carry more potential for abuse than in the matter of sex. It has been estimated that 10 – 15% of therapists have sex with clients at least once, and for some it is a regular occurrence.

I was a second-year psychiatry resident at Boston University when Susan came to our clinic and was assigned to me for therapy. Susan was twenty-four, single and very attractive. I was in my late twenties, also single and, uh, excitable. Only a few sessions into the therapy, Susan asked me to have sex with her. I can't say I had no interest, but I was thoroughly aware (at least intellectually) of how wrong it would be. I told her that I was flattered, but we were not there for sex. She didn't give up so easily. She renewed the subject at each meeting, sometimes quite insistently. Apprehensive, I talked with my supervisor, a wonderful septuagenarian who had seen it all. Again and again he helped me keep my perspective and stay on track; this included responding with respectful but firm refusals of Susan's demands.

This scene was repeated in some form at almost every session. Each time I scurried off to my supervisor and each time he hosed me down and sent me back. Finally I was reviewing my clients with him one day and I said, "You know, the last few times I've seen Susan she hasn't brought up having sex." He smiled and said, "So you've finally decided that you're not going to sleep with her."

He was right, of course. I understood all along what I needed to do, but until I convinced myself clear down to my bones, Susan was not persuaded. Her acceptance of my refusal came when I was certain of it myself.

Shortly after this she revealed a shocking history of sexual abuse, followed by painfully compulsive promiscuity as a teenager and a young woman. Early sexual abuse will often leave a girl convinced that she can be loved or valued only for sex. Susan's seductiveness with me was a repeat of all her other desperate sexual behavior. More importantly, it was an unconscious test to see if I was safe, and to find out whether I could care for her for non-sexual reasons. Had I failed the test by agreeing to her requests, I would have left her even more hopeless and desolate.

Desire and temptation are inevitable, but sexual behavior on the part of the therapist is always damaging. The therapist is in too potentially powerful and authoritative a position. There is all the power of old patterns, traumas and expectations that are carried into this relationship: I could stand in for every man who had abused or exploited Susan. There is the influence of the teacher and the healer. And there is the authority of the mother and father, for people in therapy are often seeking not only a healing guide and a redeeming spirit, but also a wise and loving parent. When powerful feelings are aroused, the client will look to the therapist for guidance. The therapist can pervert this situation to his own benefit, with whatever disastrous consequences this has for the client. The therapist may fool himself into thinking that because he cares for her, this is a relationship of equals. He may justify his coercive sexual behavior as being "good for her, because she needed to experience love," or some such rationalization. The reality is that this behavior on the part of the therapist has aspects of both incest and rape.

Boredom

The best therapy occurs when we can simultaneously monitor the client and ourselves. Our feelings, intuitions and associations often provide the very best information about what is going on.

So what about a lack of affectivity? What about boredom?

Bored in a session, I must first wonder if it is about me. Am I distracted today? Am I inattentive because I don't like this person, or because I feel frustrated? But the largest part of the time I find that it isn't me.

I'm talking with Grant for the third time. As in the first two sessions, I find myself repeatedly drifting off, having to will myself back to attention. Puzzled, I ask his permission to record the rest of the session.

When I play the tape in my peer supervision group, my colleagues fall instantly asleep. Although the content of Grant's discussion *should* be interesting, his flat tone and flatter affect gives one no purchase.

I share this with Grant at our next meeting. His immediate response is, "Yeah, everyone calls me Mr Monotone." We see how he squelches his emotions to avoid being attended to; this opens a year-long discussion of his relational fears and vulnerabilities.

Therapy is inherently interesting. People are interesting. *If I am growing bored, it is probably because nothing is happening.* Sometimes I tell a client: today I'm having difficulty staying with you. So let me ask, is this what you need to be talking about right now? He admits, perhaps self-consciously, that it isn't, and within a minute or two we are talking about something that is anything but boring.

The next most frequent cause of boredom is therapist burnout. *Burnout is a form of fatigue that results from giving more than we are getting back over a long period of time.* Burnout means running on empty. When we don't care for our own needs, when we are consistently sacrificial, when we keep trying to do more than we can do, and when we assume responsibility for other's lives, we find ourselves depleted.

We may need time off, perhaps a vacation. We may need to ask if we are creating enough space in our own lives, or getting enough rest or exercise, and if we're having any fun. Are we working too many hours, and are we receiving sufficient pay?

Above all we need to ask whether we are investing too much in the outcome, trying to take on responsibility that isn't ours. A good rule of thumb: *If you are working harder than the client, you are working too hard.* Let the client's life be his.

Shame and Guilt

Shame and guilt erupt in our work like recurring volcanoes. I suspect they are issues in everyone's therapy at some point. The distinction between shame and guilt, and the resultant therapeutic approach, is often hazy.

My etymological dictionary tells me that the word "shame" traces back to the Gothic word *skanda*, meaning disgrace (Yiddish and German *schande*, also related to the English word *scandal*.) Shame concerns the disapproval we expect from other people. Shame is public, with reference to being seen. We have done something, or we are something, that we would rather no one know about. We would be disgraced. We are judged by the standards of others, or at least what we expect their standards to be. Whatever we are ashamed of, we can handle it as long as it remains our secret, as long as no one knows.

"Guilt" comes from the Old English word *gyltig*, meaning culpable; more specifically, responsible for an offense and deserving punishment. Guilt signals our belief that we have committed a moral, not just a social, transgression. We are answerable whether or not anyone knows. Keeping quiet may avoid external punishment, but it doesn't relieve inner remorse. What we have done (or felt or thought) is dishonorably wrong, and we deserve to pay some penance.

The two can occur simultaneously: I have stolen something, and I am both guilty and ashamed. I can avoid shame if no one finds out, but I remain certain that what I have done is wrong. Guilt can be relieved by confession, reparation and forgiveness; a criminal is relieved of guilt when he has "served his debt to society". Shame, however, is about one's fundamental defects in the eyes of others, and can be dealt with only through concealment.

The toxin of shame has most of its roots in childhood, when we think that adults are all- knowing. What they tell us about ourselves must be true. If I am held to be a bad, inadequate or unlovable child, that is how I will understand myself. If I am abused, I must somehow deserve abuse.

People who grow up with shame live an ongoing struggle to be (or at least appear to be) other than they are, to seem better or less wicked or more lovable. They see criticism, rejection and abandonment lurking in every interaction. Introjecting the disapproval, they become relentlessly self-critical, living a life of chronic apprehension, hiding and dreading exposure. The only reprieve lies in presenting a false self to the world.

People don't come to therapy to do something about their shame, for they don't want to expose it, even to their therapist. They come when something else has become intolerable. Shame emerges only after we have won their trust, and then only with great trepidation. In many situations—eating disorders and sexual variances being two good examples—shame about the condition becomes itself a major part of the problem.

Since shame begins with other people, *the only antidote for shame is the experience of acceptance by another.* When the individual feels accepted, he can finally begin to think he may be acceptable; perhaps he need not change who he is in order to be adequate or lovable. This is the therapist's task: can we see and embrace this person as he is? Not necessarily for what he has done, but for who he is in his heart, including the yearnings and fears that drive him? This can be a moment of challenge for us; if our acceptance is not genuine, he will know it.

Yet, the therapist asks, isn't it our job to enable change?

And the answer is yes, of course. That is precisely the operating paradox: *no one changes until he feels accepted for the person he already is.*

Shame is about who we are. Guilt is less about who we are and more about what we do (or think or feel). With guilt there is no need for a false self. If the offense could be annulled, if we could change the deed or thought, everything would be all right.

I find it useful to differentiate two types of guilt: conscience and superego. Conscience, or relational guilt, has its genesis in compassion and empathy. I have deceived a client, or I haven't given my child the affection she needs because I have been self-absorbed. Or perhaps I have let down someone whom I owed better. It is a failure of relationship, and we have also let ourselves down.

In our freshman year of college, my old high school friend and I were invited to join a fraternity, and we both accepted. A week later his invitation was shockingly retracted, to his great embarrassment and pain. I went ahead and pledged. This was my mistake on several levels, but one in particular concerns me here: all these years later, I still regret not telling them that they couldn't reject only one of us.

There is no remedy for relational guilt. We can only use it as an opportunity to learn.

The second type is superego guilt. I use the word in its Freudian sense: a collection of rules and judgments that were imposed by others—parents, church, etc.—and that are now internalized and perceived as one's own. These may have little to do with relationship or compassion, and the guilt may be exceedingly punitive. "I'm supposed to love my parents, and I don't; I'm a terrible person." Many of society's rules about sexual behavior fall in this category of superego. Interestingly, superego guilt rarely stops us from doing what we want to do. It just makes us feel bad about it.

The therapist's task is to raise questions about the rules and their sources, to correct misinformation and to offer alternative perspectives. Thomas finds himself with occasional adulterous thoughts. Although he has never acted on them, he considers himself sinful. We engage in a broad discussion of the nature of male sexuality, its biology and psychology. He is fascinated, if incredulous, at the information that these thoughts are universal, and that the drives have served a function in the survival and perpetuation of the human species. Once he digests that, he can consider my suggestion that our actions, not our thoughts and impulses, determine our moral integrity.

Responding to his question, I tell him yes, I have many such thoughts, and I have often experienced temptation. Because I value my marriage, I have chosen not to go there. It is not temptation that makes us moral or immoral, but the decisions that we make and the actions that follow from them.

Superego speaks in a commanding roar from Mount Sinai. Conscience addresses us as a quiet voice from within.

The Treatment Plan

Successful military commanders have an axiom: No battle plan ever survives the first contact with the enemy. In medicine and in surgery, physicians' forecasts are approximations at best. Prediction is uncertain in any enterprise.

Despite this, "treatment planning" is much in vogue today. It is based on the fantasy that treatment is an emotionally disinterested process that can be arranged and predicted, that healing need not be individualized, and that relationships can be automated. The managed care industry has seized on these assertions for reasons that are too obvious.

It may remind us of Procrustes, the mythical villain who took travelers under his "hospitality" and bound them to his bed. If they were too long to fit, he cut off their feet; if too short, he stretched them on the rack.

The course of psychotherapy is necessarily personal and unique to each individual. Unless we are willing to emulate Procrustes, cutting and stretching each personality to predetermined size, therapy cannot be prescribed. Nor can it be predicted; when I think I know what is going to happen, I am constantly surprised. That's one of the delights of this work. There is no set of strategies that can encompass the infinite variability of human beings.

Any plan is at most an initial idea. *If we are sticking to the plan after the first immersion in reality, we have stopped doing psychotherapy.*

Money

Money can be a troublesome subject for therapists. We tend to be both romantics and rescuers, and it's not always easy to reconcile these inclinations with economic necessity and the realities of commerce. I speak from personal experience: whether holding a job or conducting my own practice, I have struggled not to undervalue myself financially. Each of us must deal with the individual issues of idealism, shame or self-worth that make this so troublesome.

As ethical people, we aspire always to treat others as intrinsically valuable. Must that mean that we practice our professions unmotivated by money? Must we forgo pecuniary gain in order to do this work honorably? After all, it takes money to live, and money is not a bad thing. We are not taken aback when the gardener, the photographer or the pediatrician expects to be paid for her work. It does not make the enterprise less meaningful or satisfying. We can take pleasure from what we do, approach our clients with kindness and respect, and still welcome the monetary rewards.

There is, it is true, the danger of materialism. Marketplace transactions are susceptible to greed, exploitation and callousness. And the personal nature of psychotherapy makes us especially wary of corrupting it. We want it to be "pure," innocent of unloving motives.

That's wonderfully wise, and also a bit fantastical. In justifying her support of an actor for political office, one woman told me she voted for him "because he's not a politician." In other words he's an amateur; do we really do so well when amateurs run our government?

Do you want your car fixed by an amateur or by a professional mechanic? At tax time, do you consult with an amateur accountant? Then how would we think that psychotherapists should be other than professionals?

Money can be many things: power, security, comfort, freedom, the ability to do things. It is also a necessary validation: someone is willing to pay for what we do.

Most of us do need to make a living. This is simply reality, not good or bad in itself. Money is not an evil thing, though greed often is.

Making a living is part of taking care of ourselves, and if we do not tend to it, it will contribute to resentment and burnout. It is also part of the structure of psychotherapy, providing a defining element of the relationship. However much we care, this must remain professional, with boundaries that will not be crossed.

Complex Relationships

The relationship between therapist and client is sometimes portrayed as a simple one. In one chair sits the professional, in the other the suppliant. The therapist does therapeutic stuff and the client (if motivated) is healed. That's all there is. It sounds like orthopedic surgery.

Relationships are never that straightforward. The appellatives for them (husband, patient, friend, employer, nephew) are useful references, not reality itself. Relationships are complex and overlapping: my wife may also be my friend, my business partner, my employee, my boss or even my landlord. Any relationship that is more than superficial becomes a complex one. In the course of our work as therapists, we variously inhabit roles as friend, spouse, physician, confessor and parent.

In the real world, therapists are involved in complex alliances all the time; the notion of limiting every relationship exclusively to therapeutic exchanges seems a fantasy. We run into our clients at the theater and the ball game, at our children's school functions, at the gym and at religious services. We find ourselves on the same softball team, serving jointly on committees, or attending AA meetings together. They may turn out to be our bankers, plumbers, cardiologists or local police officers. When the clients are other therapists, we are likely to encounter them at professional meetings and conferences; in my case, they sometimes attend continuing education workshops that I present.

Talking about complex relationships is a bit like running a high school sex education course: we are not advocating behavior, merely preparing for the inevitable.

Many of our professional societies and ethics boards champion an absolute (and unrealizable) ban on "dual relationships". They point out that the imbalance of power raises the potential for abuse, and in this they are certainly right. However, this pitfall should be the beginning, not the end, of our thinking on the matter.

There certainly is a power differential in therapy. The same inequality is inherent in other benevolent relationships, including parent-child and teacher-student. There is no help for this; knowledge, responsibility and competence are always authoritative. The inequality is not in itself productive of abuse; like fire, it can warm or burn. The risk of abuse stems from our inclination to use that inequity for personal gain. I differ a bit with Lord Acton: It is not power that corrupts, but the temptation to use power for exploitation and seduction.

The insistence on the monothematic "purity" of the therapeutic relationship, even in the face of its practical improbability, leads only to secrecy. Like any prohibition (alcohol, the war on drugs, prostitution), it is widely violated and dishonored. The ban largely fails to prevent the behavior, instead driving it underground and generating fear of, and contempt for, the agency that promulgates it. It nullifies the opportunity for regulation and education, and therapists are hesitant to seek supervision and consultation about complex relationships in which they find themselves.

Other reasons are given for attempting to prohibit complex relationships. The most cogent is the legitimate need for maintaining boundaries. To evaluate this caveat properly, we must be aware of the difference between boundary crossings and boundary violations. If I knock on your door and wait to be invited in, that is not a violation. Crossings can be carefully considered and negotiated, with the welfare of the client in mind. I have been invited to a number of clients' weddings; just once, because I considered it (in this case only) therapeutic, I accepted.

An important concern about complex relationships is that of confidentiality. It is sometimes supposed that any public contact will automatically violate the client's privacy. But many clients do not experience it that way, and are unlikely to do so if we behave in a discreet and considerate manner. I doubt that the therapist will be overwhelmed by an irresistible impulse to turn to the next person and say, "This is Jack. He's a client that I'm seeing about his terrible relationship with his mother."

When we are unsure how far to go, we need to read the client's signals: casual, eager, diffident, avoidant, formal, uncomfortable or friendly. The blanket avoidance of contact or lack of acknowledgment in public may be experienced as an insult or a snub, and may reinforce his ongoing sense of unworthiness. People need to be treated with flexibility and respect, both in and out of the office. Rigidity, coldness and distance are anti-relational, and constitute bad modeling.

There is a valid concern that interactions outside the office will interfere with or distort the transference, which in psychoanalytic thinking is the core of the therapy. When such an event does enter the transference, examining it in the next session can be a contributive part of the therapy. Lanie's intense desire for nurturing emerged in our discussion after she saw me at the mall walking hand-in-hand with my young daughter. On the other hand, all behaviors are not transference behaviors. Neglecting the real-time relationship and focusing only on transference interpretation reduces all life to explanation and all connection to pathology.

We find ourselves in complex relationships. We need to make them available for consultation and supervision, thus providing the opportunity to examine them in a sympathetic setting, and to maximize their benefit for client and therapist.

The key to a complex relationship is consistency, respect and benevolence. People will light fires. It is not helpful to deal with the danger of burns by forbidding stoves and fireplaces.

Saving the World

OK, here's my plan. We saturate all the waters of the earth with a contraceptive substance. Everyone becomes sterile.

In order to conceive a child, all you need do is go to your local town hall (or whatever its equivalent in your part of the world) and apply for the antidote. No one judges your application. Approval is automatic. You return three days later and are given a pill to take.

Now every child born has been consciously desired for at least three days. Each one is wanted, and therefore likely to be loved. In one generation the world is transformed.

Defining Our Profession

Today treatment is often funded (and thus controlled) by for-profit insurance companies. In this environment, the work we do is being trivialized and defined away. The emotionally and philosophically barren industrial imagination portrays "providers" as faceless interchangeable technicians applying mechanistic sets of procedures to problems in repair and maintenance. People are "covered lives" that are defective and need to be fixed, or not. This outlook precludes relationship, artistry, wisdom, empathy, kindness, and the delightful ambiguity and abundance of meaning that makes life so interesting.

It is our obligation to advocate for a responsible and compassionate vision of psychotherapy. *The notion that faceless corporations can determine what is healthy or what requires treatment must be relentlessly challenged.*

Our rightful task consists of acting in alliance with our clients to define and embrace their essential selves, and to make changes based on personal experience and the unfolding of inner nature. We have no business promoting change as defined by an avaricious management industry.

We must declare for our healing art, based on skill and wisdom, empathy and intuition; an art utilizing scientific thought but not scientifically predictable or controllable. It must be made clear that this art, like any other art, cannot be *administered*, for it functions largely in the depths of the soul. The term "managed care" must be seen for the oxymoron it is.

We must insist upon being, and being perceived as, who we really are. If we are to trust ourselves and the art we practice, it is imperative that we stand our philosophical ground. If psychotherapy is not fundamentally respectful, loving and healing, it is not worth the name.

Miscellanea

She walked on the beach as the tide went out. She was picking up starfish that had been carried ashore and throwing them, one at a time, back into the sea.

Her visitor asked what she was doing. "I'm putting these starfish back in the water. If they stay here the sun will dry them and they'll die."

The visitor looked up and down the beach. "There must be hundreds of these creatures lying on the sand," he observed. "You can throw back only a few; all the rest will die. What can a few matter?"

She bent to pick up another starfish, looked at it thoughtfully. "It matters to this one," she said, and tossed it into the water.

The Talmud tells us, "He who saves the life of a fellow human is as if he had saved all of humanity."

The artists of Japan have a marvelous custom. When they are finishing something—perhaps a piece of pottery—they deliberately leave a small flaw. This reminds them that they are artists, not gods. They say further that they are not causing the pot's lack of perfection; their visible flaw serves as a reminder of all the imperfections that we cannot see.

A Zen master was asked how things were for him now that he had attained *satori*. With a twinkle that said not to take it all too seriously, he remarked, "I still have hemorrhoids."

We are who we are. Better is possible. Perfection is a dangerous myth. I don't know what a perfect person would be like, but I'd bet on boring.

"Why must I go into this? It's too painful; what good does it do to talk about it?" Until we identify our conflicts and traumas, they sneak up and suckerpunch us. In the folk tales of many cultures, once you know the name of the demon, you can begin to control him. Rumplestiltskin comes to mind.

The only person in this world whom I have the ability to change is myself. I cannot change my partner, my children or anyone else. I cannot compel my mate to be more affectionate, sexual, accepting or interested in my welfare. I cannot coerce her into being more loving with me. I *can* ask how I might become *more lovable to her*. I can change my behavior. I can learn to be less critical or more generous, gentler or more honest or a better listener. This still will not change her, but it will *invite* her to change.

If you want to recreate a relationship, set out to change what you do.

Decisions are difficult. Often it is hard to know the right thing. We are confused by conflicting priorities. We convince ourselves that the easy way or the self-gratifying act is the correct one. We allow ourselves to be misled by other people's opinions or by our desire to please them.

But above all, decisions are difficult because there are always losses. Whenever we decide in favor of something, we give up something else. If I give you my sandwich, I can't eat it myself. When we choose a loving behavior we forgo the satisfactions of greed, self-righteousness and blaming.

We may avoid making choices, refusing to be committed, unwilling to deal with the losses. We will not settle for anything less than everything. Then the things we do will be good only for the moment. In insisting upon having it all, we have nothing for very long. There is no *yes* without a corresponding *no*.

"If he loved me, he would know what I want."

How often we hear this: when we love someone we just know how she feels, what she needs and desires.

"So you'd like him to bring you flowers sometimes. Have you told him?"

"I shouldn't have to tell him. He should know that."

"He may not know that. Think about telling him what you'd like," we suggest.

"If he really loved me, he'd understand that. Every woman likes flowers."

"Perhaps he doesn't know *you'd* like them."

"If I have to ask, it isn't worth it."

Is that your final answer? If you're not willing to ask for what you want, you're not likely to get it. People *don't* just know. You and he are different. You think and feel differently from him, act differently, have your own background, biology and experience.

The other side of this illusion occurs when we think we know what is on the other person's mind. She is late again. If I were late like that, it would be because I was miffed and wanted to teach her a lesson. Damn it, I'll just go without her. And I do.

Later I find out that she was late because that's what she does – she tends to be a few minutes late for everything. It had nothing to do with me. Had I asked, I would have understood this. But I *knew* what was going on, and I was peeved.

People habitually engage in this kind of "knowing." "You did such-and-such because you just didn't care about my needs." Could she have had any other reason? Are you sure it had anything to do with you?

Love does not make us mind readers. Love is caring, not knowing.

I can stay at my job. It offers security, corporate structure, and little challenge. Boredom and depression set in.

Or I can strike out on my own, take on something risky, maybe start my own business. Very scary.

I can stay with my current lover. I lose my self-respect and even some of my identity, but I have the table-scraps of love.

Or I can walk away. Will I ever, ever be loved? Will I always be alone?

As a therapist I can continue dealing with managed care and other health insurance. It involves endless, meaningless hassles, generating resentment and fatigue that degrade the quality of my work.

Or I can resign from the system and take control of my practice, depending on patient fees alone to make my living. It's direct, it's personal, and I do my best work. But there's no security, and every quiver, twitch, and empty space in the schedule brings the fear that the practice will collapse; surely I'll be selling sneakers at Sports Outlet.

Often in life, we get to choose between depression and anxiety. These are the only options. Each of us must decide our own stance in that dilemma.

For myself, anxiety at least lets me know that I'm alive.

Sanity is learning what your crazies are, then making them work for you.

We work so hard to avoid our feelings. We use denial, drugs, intellectualization, avoidance, and on and on. What is odd is that even the most painful things we feel never really damage us. It is all the things we do to circumvent those feelings that do us terrible harm.

Most relationships don't become permanent; nor should they. Courtship is like trying on a new coat – some fit and most don't. Enjoy the present.

We can only start from where we are. Acceptance of who I am frees me to change.

Everything I have can be taken away from me—people, possessions, my health, even my life. The one exception, the only thing in life that no one can take away, is my self-respect. I can give it away, but no one can steal it.

Losses and disappointments are inevitable as well as painful. For this we have grief. The good thing about grieving a loss or a disappointment is that we don't have to do anything to fix it.

Thich Nhat Hanh presents a wonderful vision of "living with gratitude." As the Stoics taught us, happiness depends more on perception and determination than on circumstance.

We have a notion of what it will take to make us happy. This is almost always about something outside ourselves: a job, wealth, a spouse, so forth. "I'll be happy when..."

What about the present? What would it take for you to make yourself happy now? What do you need to do today?

You always have the right to change your mind.

A client who is not doing what she thinks she "should" be doing is likely to accuse herself of laziness. But what does that mean? "Lazy" only means that you don't want what I think you should want.

Couples come to us saying they need "communications skills", as if that alone would resolve their problems. It is not just knowing how to communicate that is important; it is also *what* you communicate.

Relativity theory applies to the perceptual world as well as the physical one. What you see depends on where you are standing when you look at it.

Every cloud does not have a silver lining. Some are lined with a cheap blend of cotton and polyester.

One of life's great secrets: when you don't get what you want, find a way to be happy with what you get.

Whatever I do, everyone around me divides into three groups. One group likes what I do. A second group is unhappy about it. And the third group – the largest one – doesn't care. If I change what I do, people shuffle from one group to the other, but always there are the same three groups. I may as well do what I think is best.

Everyone's behavior and thinking makes sense, if you can just get inside their frame of reference. Our job is to find that framework and operate within it, without losing the perspective of our own.

"Yes, I am getting tired. But there's no one else to do this, and I can handle it." The fact that you *can* do something doesn't mean that it's a good idea.

People who make changes may be guilt-ridden and disappointed when they find themselves slipping into old patterns. But this is inevitable; change takes time and practice. We all slip. I define success as getting up one more time than you fall down.

The importance of raising children well cannot be exaggerated. Loving our children is not only about family or how we deal with offspring. It is also about how we re-create the human race. It is about saving ourselves by fashioning pockets of kindness and decency in an indifferent or hostile world.

Ought and *should* are usually someone else's idea of who we should be. Look up their derivations. *Ought* comes from the root word for obligation, and *should* from German *shülde*, for debt.

Chinese proverb: When you go to get revenge, first dig two graves.
The proverb is correct. Revenge is like taking poison and waiting for your enemy to die.

We see our own flaws and wonder if we are up to this job. How to counsel others when we struggle so?
Nietzsche wrote, "Some cannot loosen their own chains yet can nonetheless liberate their friends." We are just people. No one has it all together. If we had to have it all together in order to be therapists, there would be no therapists.

Pain is inevitable. Suffering is a choice.

No plan ever survives the first contact with reality. Always be prepared to reassess and improvise.

Maturity is the ability to do what is right for you, even if your parents think it's a good idea.

CHAPTER 14
PSYCHOTHERAPY AND THE SPIRIT

Debate about meaning in life is endlessly sidetracked into all or nothing extremes. Traditionalism insists that purpose is pre-existent, that the universe was called forth already possessing full metaphysical import. Postmodernism insists that purpose is impossible: we arrived by chance, and chance will someday reclaim us, the universe caring not one whit either way. What's neglected is the intermediate possibility— that our being is sacred & profound, regardless of whether there are higher forces.

Gregg Easterbrook
In *Beside Still Waters: Searching for*
Meaning in an Age of Doubt

Spirituality and Psychotherapy?

Spirituality is not about what one believes. It is about the questions one asks.

What gives life meaning? How are we connected with one another and with anything beyond ourselves? Are there values that can allow our lives to transcend mere biology? How do our religious and cultural sources address these questions? And what does all this have to do with psychotherapy?

Let's begin by reminding ourselves of the key difference between psychology and psychotherapy. Psychology is a science, albeit a "soft" one. Unable to escape the paradox that the student (the human animal) is also the object of study, it at least attempts a search for objective knowledge.

Psychotherapy, while necessarily depending on psychological understanding, has its goals in the relief of suffering and the healing of persons and relationships. Like the practice of medicine, it is based in science but is not a science; it is a branch of the art of living.

In the art of living, the life of the spirit matters deeply. We face the existential need to deal with pain, loss, mortality, and the quest for meaning in our lives. Our spiritual concerns include forgiveness, justice, compassion, connection, transcendence, mystery and awe.

Religions address these concerns through ethics, salvation, historical purpose, blessing, a mystical reaching for the divine, and so forth. Not everyone accepts these religious responses, and some are incompatible with others; but even when we reject them, we still find ourselves asking the questions.

These are issues of urgent concern; once our immediate pain begins to ebb, once we have enough to eat and are out of the cold, we begin turning to these questions of meaning. As therapists, ignoring these concerns and attending only to the "psychological" ones dismisses a huge realm of living. Whatever our personal faith (or lack of it), we owe it to ourselves and our clients to attend to these matters in our work.

In psychotherapy, our relationship with the client is the instrument, and it is also the goal. We seek relief of suffering, but beyond that we seek relatedness and meaning. Even when suffering persists—and it does—we want to imbed it in meaning and relationship.

The Language of the Dialogue

When we wish to connect with someone, we do best to address him in the language that is meaningful to him. The language of religion and spirit is most often the language of myth.

Myth does not mean fantasy or falsehood, but a particular kind of truth. Myth does not intend to be literal; it conveys psychological, spiritual or social truths. The myth of Santa Claus is one of abundance and generosity, while the myth of George Washington and the cherry tree speaks of a hoped-for integrity of character that represents Americans at our best. No one but a child is expected to think these stories are factual.

Religions have always taken spiritual questions as central themes, developing mythical and symbolic languages without which we would be voiceless. Consider this fable from Nikos Kazantzakis' compelling novel, *The Last Temptation of Christ*:

> When the kings had died, a pauper, barefoot and hungry, came and sat on the throne. 'God,' he whispered, 'the eyes of man cannot bear to look directly at the sun, for they are blinded. How then can they look directly at you? Have pity, Lord; temper your strength, turn down your splendor so that I, who am poor and afflicted, may see you.' Then—listen old man!—God became a piece of bread, a cup of cool water, a warm tunic, a hut, and in front of the hut, a woman giving suck to an infant. 'Thank you, Lord,' he whispered. 'You humbled yourself for my sake. You became bread, water, a warm tunic and my wife and son in order that I may see you. And I did see you. I bow down and worship your beloved many-faced face.

Or this sentence, from *The Soul of Christianity* by Houston Smith: "Eternity can break into the moments of our experience with lightening flashes of illumination."

How could these fertile thoughts be conveyed without the use of what is essentially religious song? Petrarch, the fifteenth century Italian writer, said,

"Theology is a poem that has God for its subject." Poetry, like song and other arts, is the language of deep human experience. Art, not science, can fully express life's wonder, pain, joy, turmoil and mystery.

Art is the language of the emotions, of experience, and of psychotherapy, because it alone expresses the fullness of life's encounters. I may offer a client interpretations regarding her feared loss of integrity in a relationship and her ambivalence about being close; this is a useful piece of psychological understanding. When I bring into the room my own trembling at the doors of intimacy, my own sense of loving terror as I enter further into relationship with her, our dialogue is suddenly infused with life as we experience our vulnerability together. Once we have achieved what we can through theory and technique, therapy can be further conducted only in the languages of poetry, metaphor, mime, storytelling, humor, movement and other art forms, forms indefinitely defined, rich in the ambiguity of experience, addressing and apprehending the inner and shared life of the *person* standing in relation to me.

The word *ambiguity* is used here not in the sense of vagueness or confusion, but denoting complexity, mystery, and above all abundance of meaning. *Abundance is an irreducible core of all intense experience.* If the search for spirit is to be true to life, we must be wary of reduction, simplification and literalism.

The stories of Scripture, for example, provide an inexhaustible source of meaning and interpretation. If this bounty is reduced to naive explanations, or literal exposition, then we destroy Scripture's richness. When its irreducible complexity is accepted, we possess transcendent pieces of poetry, magnificent sources of inspiration.

To be fully meaningful, we must let the myth speak to us in its historical, social and emotional context, attempting to re-experience the mystery and the multifaceted insight it offers.

This is difficult. Facing complexity and mystery means confronting our limitations; we run headlong into sadness, pain and mortality. Certainty is so much simpler and more comfortable than experience.

But our unwillingness to live with ambiguity can have tragic results – the political polarization of the country, the needless destruction of a marriage, the constriction of life's experience. The therapist's unwillingness to tolerate ambiguity will diminish the richness of the relationship, encourage technique at the expense of caring, and limit the growth and transformation available to both people.

Spirit and Psyche

Spiritual longings are driven by psychological motives and by transcendent ones.

Psychological motives include fear, the desire for safety and protection, attempts to conquer helplessness through entreaty of a greater power, the wish for certainty, and attempts at explanation (religion as science).

Transcendent reasons are the ones we have just been discussing: the need for meaning, coming to grips with mortality, the demand for justice in the face of innocent suffering, a longing for unity, and expressions of awe, incomprehension, reverence and gratitude.

Psychological reasons are, of course, the domain of the science of psychology. Transcendent reasons exist in the realm of theology, philosophy, art and personal experience.

Psychological and transcendent motives do not exclude each other. Freud did a remarkable job of exposing the origins of religious longing in childhood fears and traumas; the difficulty came when he said that religion was *nothing but* the result of these traumas and fears.

During synagogue worship, and in the midst of a manic episode, David had an ecstatic experience of unity with all being. He asked me later if it had been merely an illusion based on the state of his brain at the time. I could only tell him to trust his current intuition. There is no reason to think that psychological illness excludes genuine religious experience, or that an authentic religious encounter precludes pathology.

Transcendent explanations do not obviate psychological contingencies, and that gives us reason for cautious reflection. When we bring our personal spiritual experiences into the social or political realm, we must be willing always to question not only our understanding, but also our fallibility as merely human vessels.

Religion and Spirit

The word *religion* is derived from the Latin *ligare*, to bind (as in "ligature"). *Re-ligare* is to bind again, to bind strongly. The word "bind" has at least two meanings: it may signify *holding*, or it may signify *confining*.

Religion in its *holding* form serves communal functions of kinship, ritual, traditional wisdom, continuity and belonging. These are positive, loving, organizing and comforting principles. Their purposes are more social than spiritual. Religion can provide a context for the preservation and animation of the sacred; but as an institution it does not provide for the sacred itself.

When religion becomes *confining*, it binds uncertainty and anxiety by offering authority and rigidity. While *holding* religion deals with suffering by enfolding it in myth and community, authoritarian religion attempts to judge it, imprison it, or explain it away (cf. Job's "friends"). Such authority can be dead and deadening; *passionate spirituality occurs only in the heart of the free individual*. The fourteenth century churchman and mystic Meister Eckhart told us: "You should not confine yourself to just one manner of devotion, since God is to be found in no particular way. That is why they do Him wrong who take God in just one particular way. They take the way, rather than God."

The therapist's spiritual function is to help the individual break out of authoritarian confinement and find his or her way. This is, for this person, the only path that will unbind the fullness of the soul, allowing one to explore within for the mysterious, the passionate and the vital, thus liberating the loving, creative, sexual, chaotic, connecting and holy forces within. The acts of the love of self, nature and others are also the acts of our connection with the sacred.

We are not talking about goals. In matters of the spirit, there can be no goals. The quest is for spirit in motion, not for answers, control, or a place to come to rest. The experience of the sacred necessarily includes anxiety, ambiguity, uncertainty and complexity. Mystery is to be experienced and lived, not solved or answered.

When we attend to the life of the spirit, as people and as therapists, we invite our clients to do the same. Many are eager for the invitation. When they choose to respond, spirituality becomes a clinical question.

Faith and Psychotherapy

If spirituality is about questioning, what then is faith? We are accustomed to thinking of faith as an acceptance of propositions: to have faith is to believe that God is something, or does something, or wants something, or that His universe works in a particular way. The classic example is the Creed, the declaration of things to be believed.

There is another way to think of faith, one that more closely reflects our personal experience. Elie Wiesel tells of a group of Jewish men gathered in a concentration camp. Irate, they put God on trial for permitting the Holocaust; at the end of the day He is found guilty. Then they need to adjourn, for it is time for evening prayers.

This is another, perhaps more difficult, kind of faith. In Hebrew, the word *emuna* is used, which translates more accurately as fidelity. If I tell you that I am faithful to my wife, I am not telling you anything that I believe about her. I am telling you about my loyalty, my devotion, my commitment. This faith is not about propositions at all, but about holding up my end of the relationship. In this way we can live in faith when we doubt, when we do not understand, when we suffer, even when we are enraged with God, as sometimes we must be. When there is genocide, when a child dies, when we see the injustice in the world, how can we not be enraged?

In therapy, our faith task is not about belief, but about relationship, and connection, and being true. Our work is not to advocate doctrine; it is to nourish and heal the ability to love and to be faithful.

Pepper is a lovely woman, a bright and successful professional, a person of compassion and soulful values. Raised in a churchgoing home and now a long-time member of AA, her spiritual life is important to her. But she has never been able to relate to God.

Her family history is instructive. Mother was a frail and insubstantial figure who fled from life into a passive alcoholic stupor. Father, a leader in their church community, was cruel and demeaning, vindictive and degrading. While he never abused her physically (that was reserved for her brother), he continually found ways to make her feel worthless and contemptible.

Someone once said that if God is a father figure, that's because father was a god-figure. When Pepper tried to imagine God, or to pray, her father's image stopped her cold.

Then, in one of our sessions, Pepper's grandmother appeared. She was the only adult who offered Pepper love, respect and approval, the only grownup who made her feel acceptable and worthwhile. Further, when she was present

Gamma had stood up to her father, backing him firmly away from his children; it was the only time Pepper felt protected and safe. Bringing these threads together, I suggested that when she next tried to pray, she might imagine God in the image of Gamma.

A few weeks later, Pepper reported her prayer—for the first time—as an experience of communion. Then she told me of a tender memory that had come to her: Gamma had been an avid and skilled horticulturist, and people always spoke of her "abundant garden".

Our faith task is to remove obstacles, including those imposed by damaging relationships and authoritarian doctrine. It is our privilege to guide people in finding their own way.

Religion and Science

In current American society, science and religion often exist in an uneasy relationship. This has not always been the case. The thinkers of the Enlightenment, including the leaders of the American Revolution, considered themselves believers; their doubts were not with religious conviction, but with orthodox dogma. (Interestingly, this has not been a problem in the East; Buddhists and Toaists, for example, have always understood that words and images only *point to* spiritual truths.)

So here is what science has to say about God: *Absolutely Nothing.* Science explores the natural universe, the laws of matter and energy. Science does not address revelation, purpose, the goals of history, or questions of value. It says that these topics are simply outside the domain of its methodological investigation. Science does not address God one way or the other; nor does God need scientific proof ; a poor God that would be!

There is no need for ongoing conflict. It is more properly a question of complimentarity, and many scientists are believers. Spirituality and religious faith operate in the area of personal meaning, where science is mute.

Science does not prove or disprove anything about divinity, morality or the human spirit. It certainly does not tell us how to live our lives. Nevertheless, science is indispensable in our work. Psychotherapy must be informed by systematic investigation and experimentation, and by evolutionary biology, brain research, endocrinology, anthropology, and other such disciplines. Without these we are working in the dark.

Science and spirit address diverse parts of the human endeavor. They even engage different regions of the brain. Reading Scripture as science rather than as myth places us in a position that theologians have rejected at least since St. Augustin. On the other hand, the denial of the deep human significance of religious myth in the name of science urges on us a vision of life that is barren of meaning.

Spirit in Psychotherapy: Connection

Archímedes, the ancient Greek mathematician, said "Give me a lever and a place to stand, and I will move the earth." The therapeutic connection is the ground on which we stand, the fulcrum from which the lever of our personhood can move someone's world. There is no true healing until the soul of the other is joined with our own, however timidly.

The word "connection" conjures other words: compassion, attachment, devotion, kinship, empathy, kindness, tenderness, union. Connection implies responsibility, caring, wholeness and healing. It suggests to us that we are never separate, that we are part of a fabric in which everything we do has consequences. It proposes that isolation and lack of relational responsibility often signal the existential sickness of disintegration. Disintegration occasions fragmentation, disengagement, separation, divorce and division. It may fairly be said that disintegration or disconnection *is* the loss of spirit.

Lack of connection reveals itself in every form of personal and social pathology. The inability of the individual to connect is narcissistic, schizoid or autistic. In families it is fragmenting, punishing, and sometimes brutal. A sense of community is essential to any healthy society, and the loss of this common center is a clear sign of decay. Our public life will be spiritless and violent so long as we lack connection with one another and with our environment. Much of our current social policy ignores or denies connection: ruthless profiteering, environmental exploitation, and homophobic and other hate legislation provide examples.

Of all the words evoked by the thought of connection, perhaps the most powerful is *compassion*. *Passion* in its original sense means suffering. *Compassion* signifies feeling with, suffering with. Compassion is an opening in the heart, a willingness to *be with* the other, even in suffering. Is there a greater gift one could give another? The most potent healers are those who can *be with*, even in great pain, especially in despair.

The need for connection and compassion seems universal. We long for it, respond to it, and suffer over its absence. Every religion has been host to some sort of mysticism; whatever the form, at its root mysticism is an attempt to connect, to overcome the lonely exile of the ego.

The decay of connection is one way of defining human evil. Whenever our religions speak of overcoming evil, love and compassion are said to be the path. Connection is the antithesis of doing evil.

To heal a person or a group of people is to awaken and strengthen connection. Pathology and evil (not always the same thing) are irreconcilable with connection and compassion. The Talmud and the Gospels remind us repeatedly that kindness for fellow creatures *is* the love of God.

Spirit in Psychotherapy: Treading Sacred Ground

It is evening. We are sitting at our campfire at the base of Montana's Beartooth Mountain Range, fifteen men and women. We've spent the week hiking and climbing in the high country, isolated from the rest of humanity, in communion only with nature and with each other. On this last night of our journey, someone remarks regretfully that tomorrow we return to the real world. Another says, "This *is* the real world, that's just the ordinary stuff again."

Both are right, and I find myself reflecting on the movement between the sacred and the ordinary. Something touches me, and I enter holy ground where I experience the interdependence of everything, where I am seized with awe, where I can see the possibilities for blessedness and consecration in my life. Sustaining this state is beyond my ability; time re-enters my consciousness and I tumble back into the ordinary. I work, I eat, I play, and at some time I find my way back to the sacred and the cycle begins again.

We cannot maintain life only in the sacred; however we try, we find ourselves back in the everyday. This is a limitation of the human condition.

On the other hand we can choose to live continually in the mundane, paying little attention to the needs of the spirit. When we do that, we impoverish our souls. We cannot live exclusively in the holy; but we cannot live fully if we do not go there.

There are times when the therapist has a place as priest or priestess: we may serve the sacramental function of mediating between the client and what is sacred to him. In guiding someone's therapy I often experience myself as a conduit, a conductor, a channel. I know that I am not alone in encountering the sacred in the presence of the other, and in the repeated and uncanny experience of something working *through* me, something powerful, a bit frightening, and always welcome.

As we sit with our clients, we can remain alert for those moments when we enter sacred ground together. We don't control these epiphanies, can't create them or make them happen. We can only create the conditions, be alert for their occurrence, respond to the moments. These moments are mysterious, suffused with enigmas and contradictions; they are full of light and darkness, comfort and anxiety, wonder, inspiration, and irreducible uncertainties.

In the ancient world of the Greeks, Mesopotamians, Jews and Christians, the ability to heal was a sign of sacred presence. In fact, the word *heal* derives from the same root word as *whole* and *holy*. The acts of healing are truly sacred.

CHAPTER 15
THE ETHICS OF RELATIONSHIP

The Modern Project

Ethics is the branch of philosophy—sometimes called moral philosophy—that concerns itself with right and wrong, with good and evil.

These concerns may be public or personal. Public ethics overlap with religion and politics. Every religion concerns itself with how people should behave, and ethical thinking is essential in political affairs: whether to govern, how to govern, and what the aims of governing should be. Personal ethics address questions of how we treat each other and how to live the good life.

The traditional quest for ethical wisdom encompasses both the pursuit of knowledge and the search for meaning. In the ancient world knowledge and meaning were seen as identical; if we understand how things are, and what we are, then we will know how to live. Socrates told us that "to know the good is to do it". In a Christian context, the same idea prevailed through late antiquity and into the middle ages.

With the rupture of faith during the Reformation, the unity of knowledge and meaning began to break down. During the eighteenth century Enlightenment, the very conception of knowledge became questionable. Trust in established authority was increasingly called into doubt, and there was a turning to empiricism—to science, reason, evidence and experience—as primary sources of knowledge. Classically, if you wished to know how many teeth a horse had, you looked it up in Aristotle. Now people began to examine horses and count teeth.

For the first time, knowledge and meaning were seen as having different sources. Knowledge now emerged largely from empirical observation and scientific investigation. But science is concerned *only* with knowledge, not with underlying meaning. Science can tell us how to do things, but it can't tell us whether doing them is a good idea. Today's science is learning to clone living creatures, but it can't tell us whether we should do so or under what constraints. Questions of meaning are not the province of scientists; those problems are left to philosophers, theologians, and the rest of us as we try to live our lives. No amount of scientific knowledge can give us purpose.

The single most important source of meaning for Western culture lies, of course, in our Biblical heritage. In this tradition it is not empirical knowledge that is required, but understanding of Divine Will. Nonetheless, the contemporary fragmentation of religion and the secularization of Western society have made it increasingly difficult to sustain such comforting notions of absolute standards.

On the one hand we are left with pluralism, relativism and revolutionary change. Post-modern thinkers tell us that everything, even narrative, is relative to one's preferences and point of view. On the other hand the desire for certainty and the horror of the abyss give rise to conservative reactions that sometimes encourage fundamentalism and fanaticism. The "Modern Project" is an attempt to find a sense of meaning and ethics without presuming absolutes, yet without surrendering completely to moral relativity.

Ethical Sources

The boundless complexity of resolving moral dilemmas has kept philosophers, religious figures and other thinkers occupied since ancient times. To illustrate the vast scope of proposed solutions for us to think about, here is an absurdly brief sampling of some major historical ideas on the subject.

Sources of ethics and ethical systems are most often seen as being outside of, and superior to, the individual. These include divine mandates, philosophical ideals, utilitarian principles, absolute humanist imperatives, custom and tradition, and the dictates of our licensing boards. Each of these offers perspective and each bears its problems.

Philosophical ideals are embodied in Plato's Republic, Marxist theory, and other utopias. The US Constitution is a practical and political version, rooted in Enlightenment principles of natural law, self-government, and the primacy of the individual (with strong suggestions of a deist or providential God). These systems are often very appealing, but they don't stand on their own; they are referential to other ideas and values: liberty, God-given rights, justice or an overarching standard of excellence. Thomas Jefferson to the contrary, they are not really self-evident.

The Utilitarian approach is interested in the general welfare. Its greatest advocate was the nineteenth century British philosopher John Stuart Mill, who proposed that right action be determined by pursuing "the greatest good for the greatest number". This is an appealing notion in a democratic society.

Utilitarianism is also a consequentialist way of thinking, which is to say that the goodness of an act depends on its consequences. The most obvious problem here is the Law of Unintended Consequences: the results of our actions are frequently unpredictable. A second problem concerns the fate of those outside "the greatest number". What if the greatest good involves torturing a group of children? Or exterminating an ethnic minority to ensure "purity" for everyone else?

At least two approaches to ethics are based on absolute standards. The secular version relies on a rational humanist perspective: it states that there is such a thing as absolute right and wrong, and it can be found through reason. The eighteenth century German philosopher Immanuel Kant expressed this in his Categorical Imperative, which instructs us to treat each person as an end in himself, and never as a means to other ends. This, too, has great appeal, yet it carries its own difficulties. Kant would say, for example, that it never allows us to lie; "categorical" means unconditional, no exceptions. But if someone bursts wildly into my office waving a gun and demanding to know where he can find you, you can count on me to lie. Other "absolutes" must also be questioned: is there no circumstance under which violence, or even homicide, may be justified?

Absolute standards more commonly arise from divine mandate. This is as emotionally loaded and controversial a subject as any we can imagine. While many of us are personally guided by religious considerations, as a source of unquestioned injunctions it has its challenges. It must account for diverse beliefs and interpretations, and widely differing understandings of God and God's Will. It is also the case that religious standards change over time: the Bible nowhere objects to slavery, but it does tell us that loaning money at interest is sinful. Further, there are too many instances when religion is appropriated to justify the fanatic's mentality: if I am acting for God, then any course of action is permissible.

Custom and tradition account for a greater part of our moral judgment than we are ordinarily aware of, and can be elevated to near-celestial status. While accumulated wisdom is often sensible, it is constantly evolving and always worth questioning. As a basis for moral problem-solving, it leaves a lot to be desired. Contemporary sexual mores, for example, are changing rapidly, and the relevance of tradition is being disputed in the definition and meaning of both sensuality and marriage. Falling unthinkingly back on custom provides little real moral guidance.

The ethics codes of our professional boards are largely based on custom and law, with the rightful goal of protecting both public and profession. Like all sets of rules, their applicability is limited and they never obviate the need for thinking things through for ourselves. Sometimes the codes of conduct consist chiefly of collections of rules designed to head off law suits. Too many "ethics workshops" are really about covering our backs. That's an important subject and worth understanding, but it shouldn't be advertised as ethics.

There is a major exception to "ethics from the outside": an ethic of virtues (admittedly an exceedingly old-fashioned word). This way of thinking does not emphasize universal principles, like Judao-Christian or Kantian ethics, or outcomes, like Utilitarian or Marxist theory. Instead it is located within the individual. Its central question is, "What kind of person do I choose to be?" This is the sort of ethic proposed by Aristotle, Nietzsche and Sartre. It is about one's relationship with oneself and about integrity and good faith in relationship. It leads to such statements as, "I don't lie because I'm not a liar." Virtue ethics have to do with who we are, individually and in community. It assumes self-determination and personal responsibility. It is an approach that can be exceedingly useful in psychotherapeutic work. It leaves unanswered, in any objective sense, the fundamental ethical problem: On what do we base these choices? In this way of thinking, only our personal experience can tell us which decisions are best and what kind of people we want to be.

Conflicting Priorities

We see that traditional wisdom can be both useful and confusing, beset with differing and sometimes incompatible concerns and principles. As a result, ethics can't be just a list of rules. Ethics by the rules is helpful only as long as the real-life situation is specifically covered by the rules; as long as there are no ambiguities or complicating factors; as long as there is not too much interpretation involved; and as long as the rules are not in conflict with other rules, values and beliefs.

The problem of conflicting priorities is an eternal part of ethical decision-making. Recurrent questions perplex us in both ancient and modern guises. Cogent arguments have been proposed for every conceivable answer to each of the following questions:

Does a particularly important goal justify doing things that would otherwise be prohibited? Are there times when "the end justifies the means", or do bad means inevitably corrupt the ends? Is it wrong to steal food in order to feed my family? To lie in order to protect myself or someone I care about? To disobey orders when I believe my country is wrong?

If evil means have already been employed, can we still profit from the results? The Nazis gained real medical information from monstrous experiments on their victims; may we use that knowledge, or does its genesis render it too repugnant?

Are we to be judged morally by what we do, or by who we are? Judaism and Islam place their emphasis on behavior, while Christianity has generally been more interested in our motives and intentions. The Greeks held Oedipus guilty even though he did not know what he was doing; Freud insisted that what happens is what we unconsciously *wanted* to happen.

What if I aim to help but end up doing harm? Do sincerity or good intentions count? Do we judge by intent or by outcome? Our legal system tries to consider both; a crime is a crime, but the punishment is often adjusted to match the presumed motivation.

Are moral standards absolute, or sometimes relative? When is it permissible to deceive people? If a physician gives someone a placebo and that person benefits from it, is that still lying? Is it acceptable to deliberately cause pain? We might do so in self-defense, or revenge, or a state-sanctioned execution. Are there times when torture is justified by the need to extract information that might avert an act of terrorism?

Is the value of life relative or absolute? Is it right to allow someone to die when the brain no longer functions, or does that degrade the worth of life itself?

When does the fetus become an actual person, entitled to protection? At conception, at birth, or somewhere in between? (Or, as in my family, when it completes graduate school?)

We may be faced with irreconcilable obligations. In Greek myth, Orestes' mother murdered his father. How does Orestes choose between his unconditional duty to avenge his father and the equally absolute responsibility not to kill his own mother? How do we reconcile our requirement of confidentiality for our clients with our social duty to prevent serious crime? If a pharmacist is morally opposed to birth control, is he obligated to fill a prescription for contraceptives?

Finally, what is the relationship between what is legal and what is moral? What is our responsibility when the law seems unethical? Do we comply with the edict and turn in a runaway slave? May we refuse to serve when we believe a war is unjust, and what does that say to the individual who does his duty and goes anyway? What is the relationship between mercy and justice?

It would be easier if ethical decisions were simply a matter of knowing the right thing, if there just weren't so many complex considerations. Yet, on a matter-of-fact daily level, the complexity is not the hardest part. The hardest part has to do with temptation.

Temptation

All relationships involve power, and the therapeutic relationship is no exception.

People come to us looking for many things. Some are apparent: hope, an accepting presence, a wise mentor, the alleviation of pain. Other desires may be less conscious: the longing for a good parent, a respite from struggle and responsibility, perhaps a state of perfection or salvation. These wishes can invest the therapist with enormous power in the client's eyes. It may not always be true that power corrupts, but, being human, it surely presents us with temptations.

The subject of temptation returns us to familiar ground: the person of the therapist. Thinking about ethical decision-making in the abstract is, well, abstract. Ethics are personal and relational. They are about who we are. *Most ethical failures are not about knowing what is right, but about the temptation to do something else.*

We will be tempted. We want things for ourselves, as we should. We have needs and desires, passions, fascinations and obsessions. To be human is to embody compassion and cruelty, generosity and greed, grandiosity, lust, rage, kindness, tenderness, and the most horrifying violence. If we do not know this about ourselves, these qualities may control us.

I like to think that I am a loving and compassionate person. But I have sinned abundantly. I have been to war. I have worked in drug rehab facilities, in psychiatric hospitals and a maximum-security prison; no one I've met has done anything of which I am not on some level capable. The murderers, the junkies, the whores, thieves and pimps—all of them are me. Always, I am more like my clients than I am different. Avoiding evil and making ethical decisions requires recognition of these capacities and impulses. *To be an ethical person is not sim-*

ply to follow a code; it is to acknowledge and embrace the evil within us, and then make conscious decisions about what we will and will not do.

Clients make themselves vulnerable to us. They trust us to care about them and to value their welfare. They look to us to offer safety, to keep their confidences, and to accept them for who they are. Above all, they trust us not to abuse or exploit the authority they give us.

In turn, there are many things we want or hope for in our work. Some of them are legitimate: monetary returns, respect, the opportunity to do meaningful and interesting work, a sense of connection and a place in the community. Other things may come to us, but are dangerous when they become goals; these include our desires for admiration, status, gratitude and validation.

And some of our desires, if acted on in the therapy relationship, give rise to exploitative violations of trust: our cravings for financial advantage, sexual gratification, control and adulation. We all harbor at least some of these wishes; evil does not come from the outside. As Pogo said, "We have met the enemy, and he is us."

Our impulse to nurture and take care of people can present a special problem. A commendable and benign desire, it can also be damaging. The danger is overprotection; we fail to allow the client to make his own decisions, to take risks and grow from them. While this can be defended as an expression of caring, it may in fact spring from our desire to be needed, to feel indispensable, to be a celebrity in at least one person's mind.

Occasionally a client becomes a little special to us; their presence adds something extra to our day. This client is a little (or maybe a lot) more appealing than most, intellectually, sexually, by character or esteem, through identification, or in any number of other ways. We are tempted to treat them differently in ways that may not be good for them, and our professional codes provide no guidance other than an ill-defined injunction against "dual relationships". Let me suggest that these desires need not become a problem if we are conscious of them and willing to make ongoing decisions to keep our behavior in line with therapeutic concerns. First we must be attentive to the impulses themselves. When you approach the acceptable limits, there will be small signs: you find yourself giving the client an unwarranted break on the fees, or not charging for a missed session when that is your usual practice. You schedule meetings outside of normal hours, or take unusual numbers of phone calls. You dress in the morning and find yourself selecting that extra-nice shirt because he or she has an appointment that day.

The management of temptation requires an assertive awareness of our dispositions, blind spots, and countertransference occasions. This is not easy. It can happen only if we are willing to be self-reflective and unsparingly honest. There will be times when our own resources are inadequate to that task and we must depend on others, falling back on supervision, consultation and personal therapy.

Awareness is essential but not in itself sufficient. Once conscious, we have decisions to make, and these decisions call for personal and intellectual discipline. We must embrace all of ourselves: the creative and the destructive, the hateful and the loving, and everything else we find. We accept our abundant and corruptible humanity, forgiving ourselves the parts we dislike or fear. Then we thoughtfully choose which elements of ourselves we manifest in the world and which we choose to keep contained. These choices determine the difference between good and evil in our lives.

The Ethics of Relationship

We previously described psychotherapy as an undertaking of love, counting its acts as an elemental part of the healing. We reject the romantic conception of love as an emotion, characterizing it instead as a series of choices that one makes. Love is not something that happens to us, but something we do. It is an active verb, not a noun. The loving feelings *follow* the decisions.

Attention to the acts of loving can serve as a moral guide as well as a healing force. Our principal ethical caveat in psychotherapy must concern the exploitation of the client for our personal gain or satisfaction. The decisions required for behaving as a loving person effectively preclude this abuse.

When we manipulate someone for our own ends, that person is an object to us, a tool to be put to use. When we choose to be present and connected, the other becomes a fully living being in our sight. We are like him and he is like us, and we cannot help but be mindful of his well being. Compassionate behavior is a natural consequence.

Responsibility signifies a response to the actuality of this person and of our relationship with him. It is the opposite of objectifying him.

In the act of acceptance, we embrace the complexities and imperfections of the other person, welcoming her and assuming that being respected and valued is her birthright.

Finally, to be generous is to give, not to manipulate or take advantage. Generosity places profound importance on the welfare of the other.

While we can be ethical without love, the opposite is not true. By choosing to be more loving persons, we also become more ethical ones. We can be a force for good in someone's life, and in the world.

Ethical decisions occur in relationship, demanding mindfulness, presence and compassion. These qualities also become choices about how we live and what sort of people we choose to be.

In the healing endeavor, we enter into the lives of others in the most intimate ways. We travel with them through anxiety, hope, joy, rage and pain, through shame and pride, alienation, hunger and discovery. We explore tender regions that no one else may have seen. We uncover their secrets and fears, touching them in the most intimate and vulnerable places.

To do this without respect and love is truly a great sin.

APPENDIX: HEART AND SOUL IN A NUTSHELL

The Nature of Psychotherapy

There is no formula for therapy, nothing that will substitute for thoughtfulness, flexibility and creativity. No theory, system or technique can replace careful attention to the relationship.

The client will unveil things that are kept secret from the world, sometimes even secret from herself. She will expose her daydreams and nightmares, laden with longing, shame and hope. She will explore fears, doubts, joys, desires and terrors. The risk is enormous. It is an act of heroism to make herself so dangerously vulnerable.

Our very first responsibility is to provide a safe place for her to do these terrifying things.

As therapists, we begin with human nature as it is, not as someone would like it to be.

The word "crazy" comes from the Old Norse word *kraza*, meaning to crack or break. It also has a very specific usage: when it is time for a bird to come out of its egg into life, it begins pecking from the inside. The pattern of cracks that forms all along the shell is called *kraza*.

To go crazy, to have a "breakdown," is to peck out of one's shell for the purpose of emerging into life. The calling of therapy is to guide the client in constructing this new life outside the shell.

Psychology is a scientific study, while psychotherapy is a specialized form of the art of relationship. It is the difference between an objective investigation and a personal and kindhearted connection. Both are essential. To attempt psychotherapy without in-depth reference to psychological knowledge is to risk undisciplined vision, unexamined intuition, and the shattering of the other in the force of our passion. Striving to be therapeutic through science alone leaves us in an arid wasteland of disconnected intellect.

There have been attempts to make psychotherapy more 'scientific' by insisting that it is free of value judgments. But psychotherapy is about life, and human beings don't function in life without values and priorities. Otherwise there would be no reason to get up in the morning, or indeed to do anything. Science itself is not without values; it esteems knowledge, tough-mindedness, objectivity and a careful search for truth. If you offer me value-free therapy, I shall run the other way.

There is a difference between life's difficulties and the problems we create. Difficulties are part of living, some of them unavoidable: inconvenience, disappointment, grief, aging and death, among others. When we try to "solve" difficulties, we often turn them into problems. The idea of "solution-focused" therapy carries its own contradiction: good therapy is focused on clients, not on solutions.

To heal is to make whole—and also to make holy, for all three of these magical words come to us from the same root. The willingness to love is at the core of all healing, all wholeness, and all that is holy.

There are few places in life where one has the opportunity to love and be loved in a safe and sustaining refuge. At its best, family is one of these. At its best, psychotherapy is another.

It can be said that all therapy is family therapy. We bring with us all the significant people in our lives, past and present. The room is crowded with them; they teem and swarm, noisily demanding our attention. They pop up when expected and when least expected. The crowd fills the office, at times consuming all the air. They can hardly be ignored. It has been truly said that family therapy is not just about the people in the room, but about the people in the minds of therapist and client.

Another way to describe the essence of therapy is that the therapist resists enlistment in the client's and family's usual patterns; we strive to be who we are in our relationships with them, rather than participating in their problematic ways of being.

When religious and spiritual issues arise in therapy, our task is not about belief, but about relationship, and connection, and being true. Our work is not to advocate doctrine; it is to nourish and heal the ability to love and to be faithful.

Therapy Is Relationship

All healing occurs in the crucible of loving relationships, and psychotherapy is a loving relationship designed especially to facilitate that healing. Regardless of the theories and techniques employed, or the particular dynamics of any given moment, the healing always occurs in relationship. This is why so many different personalities and approaches are likely to succeed: the healing power of the connection may flow in many different channels.

What people do in their lives, they will do in the therapy relationship. When these acts and feelings emerge into consciousness in the office, they reveal the issues in a live and immediate way that nothing else can. This lends enormous experiential power to the work. Whatever else is happening in the therapy, if something bears on the relationship in the room, drop everything and pay attention. Attend to the relationship first and always.

The therapist's job is to join in a very special relationship, one that does not precisely exist anywhere else in life. In this relationship we combine aspects of healer, teacher, confessor, parent and friend. The relationship is built on caring, wisdom, instruction, astounding confidences, psychological knowledge, deep exploration and acts of love.

The therapist's responsibility is to make maximum use of herself and the therapeutic relationship, while recognizing the limitations and imperfections of life. She cannot be responsible for other people's happiness or for whether they get what they want. She must allow her clients to own their difficulties, and thus to own the resolutions.

Stated practically, our task is to be with people and to be the very best therapists we can be. The outcome is up to God, karma and the universe.

Psychotherapy is an art based in acts of loving. The loving bond works as a force for healing the psychic wounds that we all bear.

The first act of love is to be present. This means to be fully with the individual in compassion and empathy. We must be willing to journey with him through his pain, joy, fear, anger and confusion, and to tolerate a great deal of uncertainty. The therapy we can do is often limited by what we are willing to endure.

Don't just do something. Be there.

The power of the therapist's acceptance resides not only in the transference, though it may begin there. In the end, the regenerative acceptance and compassion that the client so needs can come only from an authentic human being who is willing to care in a connected and personal way.

Only through the experience of being loved do people learn that they are lovable. We can help them discover their worthiness only through our willingness to value their worth.

Resistance is not simply something one brings to the office with him. It is also relational. It is not just that "the client is being resistant." Rather, he is resistant now, with me, under these circumstances. "What does he resist?" is only half the question. The other half is "What part do I play in his resistance, and what can I do about that?"

The Person of the Therapist

The person of the therapist is the decisive element in the healing. In the most radical and fundamental sense, the therapy depends on who we are when we are with our clients.

The primary pitfall, then, is the failure to lay claim to who we genuinely are. Our first and ongoing assignment must be our own integrity. If we play a role or follow routinized and prescribed behaviors, if we respond to our clients with a lack of consciousness, if we give in to ego or greed, lust or competitiveness, we are certain to repeat some of their damaging experiences.

There must be congruence between what we do and who we are. Rules and procedures can only provide guidelines. They cannot tell us what is healing at this moment, and they cannot account for the quality of each relationship and the personalities of each therapist and client. The rules cannot make allowance for individual temperament or experience. If we practice 'by the book,' there will be many people whom we fail to help. Rigid adherence to prescribed codes and techniques discourages personal connection; without that connection there will be no authentic healing.

Caring is not easy. Caring makes us unsafe. When we care about someone we risk disappointment, anguish and loss. At the very least, we suffer their pain with them. The word *compassion* means 'to feel along with.'

The client can benefit from the therapy only by being fully available to it. And the client can be fully available only if the therapist is present for his pain, his anger and his fear.

It is understandable that we hesitate to care. It can wound us deeply. If one is unable or unwilling to suffer these wounds on a daily basis, it may be wise to consider another profession.

The best therapy occurs when we can simultaneously monitor the client and ourselves. Our feelings, intuitions and associations are often the most important indicators of what is going on.

It's fortunate that we needn't have everything right in our own lives in order to be helpful to others. If being therapists meant that we had to have it all together, there would be no therapists.

Self-Care

Taking care of oneself is perhaps the single most important ongoing function of the good therapist. Caring for oneself and for one's own needs does not imply a disregard for others, only an equal regard for oneself.

When we do not care for ourselves, we quickly become depleted. That which we give will become increasingly unproductive and barren.

It may be difficult knowing the measure of our own responsibility. This is not taught in graduate school, and most of us must learn it the hard way. One of the best means for identifying our over involvement lies in observing our own energy or fatigue.

Burnout is the fatigue that results from giving more than we are getting back over a long period of time. Burnout means running on empty. When we don't care for our own needs, when we are consistently sacrificial, when we keep trying to do more than we can do, and when we assume responsibility for others' lives, we find ourselves with little left to give.

To damage ourselves in this way is no favor to the people who turn to us. Time, energy, money, personal privacy—all must be rationed, for our resources are not limitless. Those who try to save the whole world end up being punished by it.

When I find myself having difficulty with someone's therapy, it is most often because I have not come to terms with something in my own attitudes and reactions. Self-awareness, the opportunity to recognize and manage our own responses, is the single most valuable part of consultation and supervision. We are human, with emotions and needs. Counterexperience and countertransference will occur. The important point is that we identify and manage them creatively and in the service of the therapy.

Ethics

Most ethical failures are not about knowing what is right, but about the temptation to do something else. Avoiding evil and making ethical decisions requires recognition of all of our capacities and impulses, including the ones that make us feel ashamed or embarrassed. To be an ethical person is not simply to follow a code; it is to acknowledge and embrace all that is within us, and then make conscious decisions about what we will and will not do.

Strict obedience to rules encourages rigidity, and rigidity precludes the personal dimension. No system of rules can promote the qualities of judgment and compassion, or the balancing of complex priorities. In fact, unthinking observation of rules can lead us to anti-therapeutic and even unethical behavior.

On the other hand, it is foolish to ignore the formal systems of ethics and practice, standards set by our professional boards and civic governments. Standards are necessary to protect both profession and public. Still, they carry an inherent dilemma: these standards are not exclusively concerned with ethics. They also have legal and political purposes that may or may not be congruent with the client's welfare.

Desire and temptation are inevitable, but exploitative behavior on the part of the therapist is always damaging.

Countertransference is an inevitable part of doing therapy. The critical question, both therapeutically and ethically, is whether we identify it and use it in the service of the client.

Ethics can never be an add-on, an empty following of rules. As blood supplies the body, true ethics is animated by consciousness within the relationship. It is a fundamental part of good therapy.

ABOUT THE AUTHOR

Stephen Howard, MD, has spent almost forty years in the practice of psychiatry, psychotherapy and family therapy. He is a popular teacher and speaker, and has written extensively for magazines and journals.

He has worked in settings as diverse as drug rehabilitation, hospital psychiatry, the U.S. Marine Corps in Viet Nam, and his current office practice in Atlanta, Georgia. This book is not a compilation of research or a collection of prescriptions, but an attempt to convey the wisdom acquired in a long and gratifying career.

His lifelong interests in philosophy, history and religion lend a unique approach and broad appeal to his psychotherapeutic writing. At a time when many advocate prescriptive and formulaic approaches to therapy, Dr Howard explores the powerful and intimate relationship of psychotherapist and client, showing how attention to this interaction can guide the therapeutic work. Since it is the relationship that provides the opportunity and context for change, it is the therapist's use of self within that relationship that makes possible the conditions for healing. The relationship and the use of self are explored here in language that is clear, engaging and at times lyrical.

He lives and works in Atlanta. He has been married to Arlene for 35 years, has a daughter Marisa and a daughter-in-law Isadora, and is a new grandfather to Emmett. Sometimes he wishes he were two inches taller.

Please see the author's Website at www.stephenhowardmd.com

INDEX

CPSIA information can be obtained at www.ICGtesting.com
261675BV00002B/1/P

9 780761 840121